". . . and the face of Christ,
there represented,
seemed to us more true,
more profound, more human and divine,
than any other image . . ."

—Pope Paul VI

The Shroud of Turin is a 2,000-year-old linen cloth which bears the imprint of a man's pain-wracked body. *The Sacred Shroud* is the story of its origins, its authentication, and the gradual unraveling of the mysteries surrounding it. It is not a painting. It is like nothing else on earth. And, in the light of mounting archaeological and scientific evidence, it may prove to be the greatest of all miracles—a self-portrait of Jesus Christ.

"An amazingly detailed picture of a bearded man who had been beaten about the body, crowned with thorns and pierced with nails through the wrists and feet. . . . Of all the reputed relics of Christ's crucifixion, none holds more fascination for believers and skeptics alike than the mysterious 'Holy Shroud of Turin.'"

—*Newsweek*

THE SACRED SHROUD

by Thomas Humber

*(A revision of the book
originally published under the
title: The Fifth Gospel:
The Miracle of the Holy Shroud)*

PUBLISHED BY POCKET BOOKS NEW YORK

POCKET BOOKS, a Simon & Schuster division of
GULF & WESTERN CORPORATION
1230 Avenue of the Americas, New York, N.Y. 10020

The Sacred Shroud is a revised and up-dated version of *The Fifth Gospel: The Miracle of the Holy Shroud.*

ISBN: 0-671-41889-0

First Pocket Books printing January, 1978

10 9 8 7 6 5 4

POCKET and colophon are trademarks of Simon & Schuster.

Printed in the U.S.A.

To Lorrel and Christopher
who endure

Acknowledgments

I am neither a scholar nor a scientist, and this book is largely the product of secondary research, an attempt to present clearly in one accessible volume the complex story of the Shroud of Turin. In this task, I have been amply aided by those who have gone before, largely unheralded in the eyes of the general public. I am particularly indebted to the research and writings of John Walsh, Dr. Paul Joseph Vignon, Dr. Pierre Barbet, Professor Werner Bulst, Dr. David Willis, the Reverend Edward A. Wuenschel and the Reverend Maurus Green. Without the remarkable photographs of Secondo Pia and Giuseppe Enrie, the Shroud might never have been studied at all.

Words can never sufficiently express my appreciation to the Reverend Peter M. Rinaldi, who gave his time, his wisdom and his aid at every step, often sacrificing his own important work. The fact that the Shroud of Turin is known at all in this country is largely due to the efforts of Father

Rinaldi and the Reverend Adam J. Otterbein, and for that we should all be thankful to them.

If this book has any originality or importance at all, the efforts of Peter A. Tscherning deserve much of the credit. His ability as a linguist, his tenacity as a researcher and his brilliance as a scholar made a frighteningly complicated task manageable.

On March 23 and 24, 1977, the first United States Conference of Research on the Shroud of Turin was held in Albuquerque, New Mexico. To the two men—Dr. John Jackson and Dr. Eric Jumper—whose groundbreaking collaborative work has thrust the study of the Shroud into the area of space-age science and whose tireless energy spearheaded the conference, I extend my special thanks. Thanks also to the following participants and researchers whose own work, presentations, personal discussions and/or correspondence have enabled me to revise the book with the latest and most authoritative information available: Joseph Accetta, Dr. Robert Bucklin, Don Devan, the Reverend Dr. Robert Dinegar, the Reverend Francis Filas, Donald Janney, Jean Lorre, Donald Lynn, Thomas McCown, Dr. Walter C. McCrone, Roger Morris, Bill Mottern, Dr. Mary Elizabeth Patrizi, Monsignor Giulio Ricci, the Right Reverend Dr. John Robinson, Ray Rogers, David Rolfe, the Reverend H. David Sox, Charles Webb, Ian Wilson and the members of Christ Brotherhood.

These people have either knowingly or unknowingly contributed to my ability to write this book. They are not, however, in any way responsible for any misinterpretations or factual inaccuracies into which I might have blundered, nor should my acknowledgment of their contributions be taken to mean that any of them subscribes to either my presentation or conclusions.

Author's Note

When the first edition of this work was published in December 1974, it was issued under the title *The Fifth Gospel*, a phrase that has been commonly used to describe the Shroud of Turin because of its graphic depiction of the Passion of Jesus Christ and its amplification of the written Gospels.

That title has been changed for two reasons.

First, as pointed out by Thomas Paterson of Christ Brotherhood in Santa Fe, New Mexico, it is possible that some readers may associate "The Fifth Gospel" with the so-called *Gospel According to Thomas*, a collection of gnostic writings reputed to have recorded the sayings of Jesus.

Second, I have since learned that a man named Hans Naber, who has published several texts on the Shroud, used *The Fifth Gospel* as the title of one of his publications, and I wish no misidentification with the aforementioned or his work.

Throughout this book, the words "images," "stains," "imprints" and "markings" are used—often interchangeably—to describe the appearance of the body and wounds visible on the Shroud. Such use is strictly for descriptive convenience, since the actual, physical means by which the Shroud picture was formed is presently unknown.

Readers interested in obtaining reproductions of

Shroud photographs may do so by requesting a price list from: The Holy Shroud Guild, 294 East 150th Street, Bronx, N.Y. 10451.

Copies of the *Proceedings of the 1977 United States Conference of Research on the Shroud of Turin* are available from the same source.

Contents

Introduction

For over six hundred years, an international storm of controversy has raged over an ancient strip of linen known simply as the Shroud of Turin. Thousands of books and articles have been written about it. Millions of people have made the pilgrimage to see it on those rare occasions when it has been exposed to public view.

The Shroud, photographs of it and its fragmentary history have been studied by scholars, historians, scientists of many disciplines, artists, textile experts and self-proclaimed authorities. It has been attacked by religious men of great faith, and it has been defended with equal, if not greater, vehemence by confirmed agnostics.

Regardless of the attention it has received, the Shroud remains virtually unknown in the English-speaking world, and its essential mysteries remain unsolved to this date. Is this remarkable cloth —with its clearly visible images of a man who was scourged mercilessly, humiliated by a crown of thorns, forced to bear his own cross, and finally crucified and gashed in his side to assure his death, all in accord with the Gospel descriptions of the Holy Passion—is this yellowed cloth the true burial shroud of Jesus Christ? Or is it the most ingenious and perplexing forgery the world has ever seen?

If it is authentic, the Holy Shroud is unquestionably the greatest religious relic known to Christianity and one of the most fascinating antiquities known to mankind. If it is authentic, the Shroud can rightfully take its place as "The Fifth Gospel," for what it reveals of Jesus and his suffering far exceeds the scant Gospel words of the evangelists. If it is authentic, and if no completely satisfactory natural explanation can account for its unusual physical properties, then the Shroud is indeed the most miraculous of Holy Miracles—an enduring, self-made portrait of the man who would be called Savior by millions of Christians throughout the world.

But what if the Shroud is a forgery, whether perpetrated for good or evil? Do we merely write it off as a clever hoax and forget it? I think not, for if the Shroud is a fake, then whoever fabricated it, by whatever unknown methods, had command of knowledge and abilities quite incredible for his time. Specifically he must have known the precise methods of crucifixion of the period; he must have possessed the medical knowledge of a contemporary master surgeon; he must have utilized an art process unknown to any great master, never duplicated before or since; he must have been able to foresee and approximate principles of photographic negativity not otherwise discovered for centuries. He must have used a coloring agent that would be unaffected by intense heat. He must have been able to incorporate into his work recently discovered details that the human eye cannot see and that are visible only with the most advanced computer-scanning devices. He must have been able to reproduce flawlessly, on a nearly flat linen surface, in a single color, undistorted three-dimensional characteristics of a human body.

All of this had to have been done prior to 1356, for since that date the Shroud has a clearly documented and uninterrupted history. Impossible? Probably, but so, by some lights, are the statues of Easter Island, the construction of the ancient pyramids and the astronomical calculations of Stonehenge. Even now, with all the scientific knowledge and technical skills at our command, the Shroud cannot be satisfactorily duplicated.

For many people, it may well be easier to accept the authenticity of the Shroud than to face the almost insoluble mysteries it would present were it a fake. Two thousand years of Christian tradition is strong medicine, and even the most hardened skeptics have not been able to deny the historicity of Jesus or his crucifixion. What then, believers will ask, is so difficult about accepting the existence of a visible record of Jesus' last hours?

There are others who will be like Thomas, the doubting disciple. They will want to believe, but they must be shown; they must have tangible proof. To still others, the Shroud will not be a religious question at all, but a problem for science and archaeology, a challenge to the ability of contemporary man to gradually erase, one by one, the mysteries of the past so that he may better understand his future.

Regardless of prior orientation, the story of the Shroud is a fascinating one to Christian, agnostic and atheist alike. But why, then, if the Shroud is so important, if the controversy over it has been

so great, has it remained so obscure? Why have
most people never heard of it, and if so, only
vaguely? Why are the details of this centuries-old
puzzle just now beginning to achieve the public
prominence and study they deserve? Although
they cannot easily be justified, there are ample
reasons.

Primary among these is the fact that, prior to
November 1973, the Shroud had been on public
display only twice in this century—in 1931 and in
1933—and then only for a few days' duration. At
all other times it has been kept hidden away—
wrapped around a wooden pole, ensconced in a
long, silver reliquary—in a vault of the Royal
Chapel behind the chancel of the Cathedral of
Turin, Italy.

Although actually owned by Humbert II (Umberto) of Savoy, the exiled king of Italy, the
Shroud has for centuries been under the care and
supervision of the Archdiocese of Turin. And until
very recently the hierarchy of the church had been
strangely indisposed toward allowing sophisticated
scientific investigation or any extended public display of the Shroud. The reasons for their reluc-
tance can only be a matter of conjecture, since
their intransigence has been equaled only by their
silence. Suffice it to say, however, that their greatest sin has been one of benign neglect, for no one
who is knowledgeable seriously believes in any
conspiracy of suppression, as has been charged
from some quarters.

Contributing to the Shroud's obscurity is the fact
that in the early years of this century, several
scathing attacks on its authenticity by reputable
scholars in prestigious publications were potent
enough to severely stifle public interest. That these

scholars based their dismissals of the Shroud as a fraud solely on several historical documents of dubious validity, completely ignoring the more legitimate results of scientific inquiry, did little to alleviate the damage.

The final reason for our lack of knowledge concerns the general inaccessibility of information about the Shroud. Although books and articles on the subject number in the thousands, few have been popularly written and published, and only a handful have appeared in English. Some of them, of course, have been the works of crackpots and charlatans, to be immediately dismissed; others the efforts of men who found only what they sought, and who sought to make their genius more compelling than their evidence.

There are several seminal works that reveal prodigious research and tireless years of devotion to the subject. I am deeply indebted to the authors of these, for without their pioneering efforts, the Shroud would probably not have achieved the recognition it has, and without their descriptions of their findings this book would have been impossible. But by and large, these books and articles were not written for, nor have they reached, the massive general audience that the Shroud demands.

The Sacred Shroud is an attempt to fill that void, to present a comprehensive yet lucid chronicle and appraisal of the Shroud to the widest possible audience. It is not an easy task, for to deal with the Shroud is to be catapulted into the complex worlds of archaeology, linguistics, exegesis, science, medicine, photography and history—all at the same time. The author can claim no particular authority in any of these fields; he is but a reporter who has sought first to understand the facts himself, and then to present them simply and fairly, without distortion. This, then, is a book for laymen by a layman.

It is purposefully not a book for scholars or critics; to discuss every critical or historical issue related to the Shroud would be to sacrifice clarity and readability, to produce a book so ponderous and so loaded with obscure references and petty detail that its goal would have been lost at the outset.

On November 23, 1973, the Shroud of Turin was placed on limited exposition, via television, throughout parts of Europe and South America. Following that showing, an international commission of scientists and scholars was allowed to examine the Shroud along with some threads and fragments excised from it. Unfortunately, the commission was severely limited by lack of proper preparation and by insufficient time. It must also be stated that, by and large, the members of the commission possessed neither the highly sophisticated knowledge nor the complex testing equipment and methodology necessary to authenticate the Shroud. Their tests must be considered rudimentary at best, and the commission's report, published in January 1976, added very little to our knowledge of the Shroud. In addition, several of the monographs included in the report proved so uninformed that the Turin authorities authorized and published a critique of their own commission's report.

Since 1973, however, a whole new breed of Shroud researchers has thrust the study of the Shroud into the area of space-age science. Several new discoveries—most notably those based on the collaborative efforts of Dr. John Jackson and Dr. Eric Jumper—are of great significance, and preparations have begun for a series of tests that should answer numerous questions about the physical properties of the ancient cloth.

An international congress on the Shroud and a public exposition of it in Turin have been scheduled for May 1978. *The Silent Witness*, a documentary film produced by David Rolfe, is also scheduled for worldwide release in May. Before that time, it is mandatory that the Archdiocese of Turin recognize its responsibility to the whole of Christianity, to history and to science and allow the necessary testing to be conducted—by people who have the scientific training to do it without mistakes and without bias.

Until the results of those tests are known, it is hoped that this book will provide the most complete, up-to-date and responsible knowledge of the Shroud of Turin.

—T.H.
October 1977

I

The "Photograph" of Jesus

The elaborate ceremony of displaying the Shroud
had taken almost two hours. Mass had been said.
One by one, the three locks securing its resting
place had been opened. The seals on its outer box
had been broken, the relic carefully extracted from
its silver casket, unrolled and attached to its back-
ing board and placed in its ornate frame. Now,
the audience—royalty, church hierarchy, foreign
dignitaries and privileged laymen—stared with
rapt attention at the ancient cloth which hung
above the marble altar in the magnificently appointed Cathedral of Saint John the Baptist in
Turin, Italy.

Archbishop Agostino Richelmy slowly took his
place in the pulpit. With his arms reverently
raised to the enshrined cloth, he began to speak:
"Behold above the altar the eternal monument to
the sufferings of God crucified . . . come to look
upon it, ye who adore the sublime beauty of
Christianity; see how the ancient prophecy is ful-
filled before our gaze. Immense is our good fortune
that we have here this Holy Shroud . . . centuries
have passed, the face of the earth has changed,
yet the honors rendered to this sacred sheet have
never ceased. . . . It is, of course, stained with
blood . . . it describes His torment . . . it reveals

His wounds. Come and gaze; kneel down and pray; let tears stream unchecked from your eyes. Peter and John found this sacred sheet folded carefully inside the empty tomb. . . . I declare that in Thee, Most Sacred Shroud, the greatest of treasures was enclosed . . . for Thou didst enfold the divine Author of our Redemption."

It was May 25, 1898, and cities all over Italy were celebrating the fiftieth anniversary of the constitution of Sardinia, on which the laws of Italy were based. But no other city possessed so great an attraction as the Shroud of Turin, and during the eight days it would remain on public exposition, almost a million people would pass beneath it to offer their veneration. Although Archbishop Richelmy had seen it for the first time when it had been removed from its storage place that morning, his sermon left no room for doubt. He believed completely in the authenticity of the Shroud. It was as if no controversy had ever existed or would be likely in the future.

For centuries, observers of the Shroud had been able to see with the naked eye the images—both frontal and dorsal—of a man who had been beaten, crowned with thorns, gashed in his side and crucified. Although the images were vague and seemingly distorted—appearing as a series of reddish brown blotches running the length of the yellowed linen—the trained eye had little difficulty discerning what they depicted. Smaller stains of a richer color indicated the wounds and the flow of blood (see Plate 4). Some observers of the time believed that the images were impressions made by direct contact of the cloth with Christ's battered and bleeding body; others, who thought the Shroud merely an artistic representation of

Christ's burial cloth, insisted that the images had
been painted on. Standing outside the cathedral
on that spring morning in 1898, however, was a
man whose discovery of the true nature of the
images would thrust the study of the Shroud into
the modern world and begin a furor that has not
yet ceased.

Like most of those who have dealt intimately
with the Shroud, Secondo Pia was an unusual
man of substantial professional accomplishments
and diverse avocational pursuits. A native of the
Piedmont region (of which Turin is the capital),
he was born in Asti in 1855. The affluence of his
family made any career possible, and he first
entered the practice of law. Later, while still in
his thirties, he made the almost obligatory shift,
for a man of his background, into local politics.
He permitted neither profession, however, to dis-
tract him from his special interests—experiments
in chemistry and physics, the serious study of
the region's art and culture and an almost ob-
sessional devotion to the then new science of
photography.

Completely self-taught and something of a local
pioneer in the intriguing new field, Pia had, by
1898, become a consummate technician, frequently improvising with his skills to compensate for
the primitive photographic equipment available at
the time. He did everything himself, from setting
up his cumbersome camera to developing, mounting and framing his pictures. The one thing he
never did, he often declared, was to retouch a
negative.

No one knows now exactly whose idea it was
for Pia to photograph the Shroud during the expo-

sition. It is known only that he had been named
to supervise a display of regional sacred art as
part of the general festivities. But certainly he
must have realized the importance and distinction
attached to taking the first photograph of perhaps
the most precious, definitely the most thought-
provoking, relic known to the church. Regardless
of the initial motivation, once the subject had been
broached, the technical challenge alone would
have compelled Pia to demonstrate his abilities.

At first Humbert I, king of Italy and nominal
owner of the Shroud, opposed the photographing
of it on the grounds that reproducing the sacred
object in such a way would diminish the reverence
and devotion accorded the relic. However, his
opposition eventually dissipated, and Pia was
given authorization to proceed, but only under the
condition that his activities would in no way dis-
rupt the exposition.

With today's sophisticated equipment, such re-
strictions would elicit perhaps no more than a
fleeting shrug from a photographer, but for Pia
they posed considerable problems. There were
only two scheduled breaks in the proceedings that
would allow sufficient time for his task.

Pia made his first attempt on the afternoon of
May 25. With the aid of several helpers, he as-
sembled a specially designed, collapsible scaffolding that would enable him to photograph the
Shroud from the proper position. Floodlights diffused by ground-glass screens were used to provide adequate light. Pia planned two exposures,
one of fourteen minutes and another of twenty.
Yet, after all his careful planning and time-con-
suming preparation, the heat of the lights proved
too great for the glass screens, which shattered

several minutes into Pia's first exposure. There was nothing to do but tear down all his equipment and wait for his second, and last available, opportunity, on the evening of the twenty-eighth.

By this time, Princess Clotilde had insisted that a special glass plate cover the Shroud to protect it from the heat of the lights. The glass would cast distracting reflections into Pia's lens. In addition, someone had stolen the bolts necessary to erect the scaffolding. Nonetheless, after two hours of preparation, Pia was ready. He was successful in obtaining both exposures without incident.

Although he had set up a temporary darkroom in the sacristy at the rear of the cathedral, Pia decided against using it, opting instead for the familiar comfort of his darkroom at home, only several minutes away.

Accounts of exactly what happened next are scarce, but the most definitive and detailed appears in *The Shroud* by John Walsh. Based on several years of extensive research, Walsh's book presents definitive reconstructions of the most important studies of the Shroud, as well as excellent portraits of most of the men central to the Shroud controversy. Here follows his account of Pia's development of his plates:

A small, red light shone feebly in Pia's darkroom as he gingerly placed the large glass plates in a solution of oxalate of iron. When the first vague outlines began to appear under the shimmering liquid, the anxiety left Pia's eyes and the frustrations of the past few days began to lift. At least there was something.

In the dim, red glare, he held the dripping

plate up before his eyes. Clearly visible was
the upper part of the altar with the huge
frame above it containing the relic. But the
brown stain-image seemed somehow different from the way it looked on the cloth itself. It had taken on a molding . . . a depth
. . . a definition. Turning the plate on its
side, he gazed at the face. What he saw made
his hands tremble and the wet plate slipped,
almost dropping to the floor. The face, with
eyes closed, had become startlingly real.

"Shut up in my darkroom," Pia wrote later,
"all intent on my work, I experienced a very
strong emotion when, during the development, I saw for the first time the Holy Face
appear on the plate, with such clarity that I
was dumbfounded by it." All his life Pia was
to remember that moment, speaking of it as
a great glory. An emotional man under his
old-fashioned reserve, his eyes were often wet
after relating the details to a spellbound
audience. More than once in these talks, he
spoke of the "trepidation" that had seized him
and made him tremble.

His first reaction to the unexpected sight
in the negative, however, had been mixed
with uncertainty. What he saw violated all
the laws of photography and he knew it.

The stain-image, diffuse and flat on the
relic, now stood out like a picture of an
actual body, the contours indicated by minute gradations of shading. The face, so
bizarre when viewed on the cloth, had become
a harmonious, recognizable portrait of a
bearded man with long hair. Emotions frozen
in death emanated from the features; a vast

patience, a noble resignation spoke out of the countenance. Even with the eyes shut, the face was suffused by an expression of majesty, impossible to analyze. All this on his *negative* plate [see Plate 5]!

Pia knew that in any negative there should be only a rearrangement of lights and shadows and a reversal of position. Light areas should become dark and dark areas light. Left should be right and right, left. The result should have been the usual grotesque caricature of the original that would make good sense only when printed in positive. Instead, here in his negative was a positive as real as any Pia had ever seen.

As he carefully lowered the plate into a fixative bath of hyposulphate of soda, he turned over in his mind the possible answers to the phenomenon. Had there been some kind of rare photographic accident, something never before encountered? Perhaps some strange property of lighting or camera could account for it. But Pia was an expert with a confidence born of a quarter of a century of experience; he had a sure grasp of photographic principle. He soon rejected any explanation but the obvious one: what showed on the negative was exactly what his camera had seen on the cloth. It was still dark on the morning of the twenty-ninth when he hastily wrote a short note to Baron Manno to announce the success of his undertaking. He didn't mention the unexpected discovery in this note; that news he would convey personally.

Later that morning, with a positive print

made from the negative, he compared the two. There was no longer any doubt. This incredible portrait existed in the stain-image. Although to the naked eye the brownish stains on the relic presented only haphazard outlines, they must, in reality, form a negative, or at least they must possess, in some mysterious way, the qualities of a negative. Thus, when a picture is taken of the cloth, and the negative plate developed, the stain-image is reversed in light values and relative position and shows positive characteristics. Exactly the same process would occur if a picture were taken of a real photographic negative.

As dawn crept through the streets of Turin, Pia sat before the negative and its print. occupied with a sudden, stunning thought. No human being could have painted this negative that lies hidden in the stains. . . . If it was not painted, not made by human hands. then . . . gazing fixedly, Pia felt a numbing certitude that he was looking on the face of Jesus.

Before Secondo Pia's remarkable discovery, believers had believed that the Shroud was authentic, and skeptics had scoffed at it. But since the Shroud had been exposed to view so infrequently during the almost six hundred years of its documented existence. there had been little reasonable basis for any opinion. The earlier squabbles about where the Shroud had originated and what it really was seem to have been conducted on a somewhat lofty plane within the church hierarchy and had little impact on the public at large.

Pia's photograph changed all that, and the world press had a field day with the story. Requests for copies of the photograph flooded in, and investigative work by scholars and scientists began in earnest. For his part, Pia was for a time attacked and vilified as the perpetrator of a cruel and sacrilegious hoax. Finally he was upheld.

It seemed that neither the church nor the House of Savoy wanted the publicity or the controversy. At the end of the exposition, on June 2, 1898, the Shroud was returned to its silver casket and stored in its triple-locked crypt. All requests for further examination were either denied or ignored. The Shroud would not again see the light of day until 1931.

II

What the Shroud Is

The Shroud of Turin does exist. It is a long strip of cloth, of which the most commonly agreed upon measurements are fourteen feet, three inches long, and three feet, seven inches wide. (The fact that even its dimensions have been contested is but another example of how restricted the access to it has been.) Although the cloth is creased and yellowed, it is still supple and, for the most part, well preserved. It is made of pure linen, woven in a herringbone pattern in what is referred to as a three-to-one twill—that is, the weft, or horizontal, thread passes alternately over three and under one of the warp, or vertical, threads (see Plate 3).

According to Virginio Timossi, the textile expert who examined it in 1931, the Shroud bears many signs of primitive manufacture, including irregularities in the pattern and imperfections in the weave. These observations have been confirmed by Professor Silvio Curto, superintendent of the Museum of Egyptology in Turin, who was a member of the commission that examined the Shroud in 1973. Professor G. Raes, director of the Gand Institute of Textile Technology in Ghent, Belgium, examined several samples excised from the Shroud as well as microphotographs of it. He, too, concluded that the linen was made in ancient times.

Laboratory tests conducted by Professor Raes showed traces of cotton fiber, indicating that the linen Shroud was woven on a loom that also had been used for weaving cotton. The cotton fibers are of a type textile authorities call Herbaceum, which was commonly used in the Middle East during the time of Christ.

Dr. William Geilmann, another textile authority and a professor at the University of Mainz, Germany, authenticated a number of similar linen fabrics, all of which reliably date from the first to the third century. One of Dr. Geilmann's fabrics is woven in exactly the same pattern as that of the Shroud of Turin.

Linen cloths of similar dimensions were woven by the ancient Egyptians. According to Professor Curto, all Egyptian cloth was made of linen until the third century A.D. It is said that the Jews learned the art of weaving during their captivity in Egypt and that they practiced the craft so well that Jewish cloth was often preferred to that of the Egyptians.

In Palestine itself, no cloth is known to have been preserved because of the extremely humid climate. Burial shrouds would have normally been destroyed quickly by the decomposition of the bodies they covered. In Egypt, however, the mummification of the body and the application of numerous bandages and wrappings have ensured the preservation of some funeral cloths. Cloths resembling the Shroud and dating from the Greco-Roman period have been preserved at Dura-Europos, in Syria.

There is no evidence to the contrary that linen

of this kind was, in fact, used in Palestine at the time of Christ. But since the use of twill weaves spanned so many centuries, the age of the Shroud cannot be conclusively determined on the basis of fabric comparisons. There is no evidence, however, that the twill weave was used in France either shortly before or during the fourteenth century—when the Shroud turned up there—and this poses severe obstructions to the critics who argue that the Shroud is a forgery of that period.

Thus, until carbon-14 or some other scientifically acceptable dating process is administered (this will be discussed in more detail later), there is only circumstantial evidence that the linen of the Shroud could date to the time of Christ.

The most striking, and disconcerting, feature of the Shroud is the two lines of black spots and white triangles that runs the length of the cloth. The black spots and lines are the traces of a fire that burned down the Holy Chapel of Chambéry, France, in 1532 and nearly destroyed the Shroud. It was kept folded in a silver casket, from which a drop of molten metal fell, burning the cloth in a symmetrical pattern. The white triangles are patches sewn on to replace areas that were completely consumed. The faintly visible pattern of lozenge-shaped stains was left by water that was thrown on the relic to extinguish the fire. Repairs were made by the Poor Clares (nuns) of Chambéry, who also sewed a piece of cloth onto the back of the Shroud. This was replaced during the nineteenth century by Princess Clotilde of Italy, who, it is said, sewed every stitch with her own hands and never rose from her knees while fulfilling the task.

On one side of the Shroud is sewn a strip of linen, about six inches wide, which runs the entire length of the cloth. The weave of this strip is identical to the herringbone of the Shroud, although why, when and by whom it was added is unknown.

Two groups of small, dark circles, visible especially at the level of the loins on the dorsal image, suggest fire damage that took place under different circumstances. Since these are reproduced on a copy of the Shroud executed in 1516 and attributed to Albrecht Dürer, the indication is that the Shroud must have been involved in another, earlier fire of which there is no record. There is, however, another interpretation of these markings, as we will see in a subsequent chapter.

Between the two lines of burns and patches are two images of a human body, one frontal and one dorsal. The length of the frontal image is 6.7257 feet; the dorsal image is 6.8596 feet. The difference is slightly greater than an inch and a half, and it can be explained by the effects of rigor mortis pulling the chin toward the chest, thus slightly reducing the length of the frontal image. (The dimensions of the images should not be confused with the actual length of the body—thought to be about five feet, ten inches—since the feet are outstretched.) The two images lie head to head, separated by a space which, while bearing no signs of an image, would approximate the size of the crown of a man's head. A sixteenth-century painting by the artist Clovio depicts the manner in which the Shroud must have been wrapped lengthwise around the body for the images to have been formed in this way (see Plate 8).

The stains that make up the images are of two distinct types and colors: the stains that comprise the images of the body are sepia-toned, with a touch of yellow ocher; the stains believed to be blood are a darker brown, with the exception of two, which are a rich carmine in color. On the Shroud itself, the bloodstains appear as positive images, while the body appears as a negative one. On the negative photograph, the body appears as positive, while the bloodstains take on negative characteristics. The implication of this disparity is that the two types of stains were transferred onto the cloth in different ways: the bloodstains by direct contact, and the body images by some sort of projection.

The images of the body are formed by continuous, mistlike stains. According to the testimony of the Poor Clares, the imprints appear on the reverse side of the Shroud with almost equal clarity, and until 1973 it was believed that the stains completely penetrated the thread of the fabric. That year an international commission of scientists conducted microscopic examinations of excised threads. They found that the stains (at least on those threads and fibers examined) are quite superficial, with virtually no penetration. This finding—the most significant one made by the 1973 commission—has important ramifications concerning the cause of the images, as we shall see later.

The stains have no sharp lines of demarcation; at the edges of the images the color gradually fades away. The delicate shading of the imprints allows the observer to discern, with some clarity, the contours of the body. Protruding masses leave a dark imprint, while depressions, hollows and crevices are indicated by a much lighter coloration. The subtlety of the images becomes much more apparent on the negative photograph than on the Shroud itself.

The face on the frontal image is reproduced with particular clarity (see Plate 1). The hair, the mustache, the beard, the orbital ridges, the nose and the lips stand out quite distinctly. The left side of the face (also to an observer's left since an image is reversed on a negative photograph) made a much heavier imprint than the right side did, and in the negative photograph it looks swollen, as though it had been struck. Traces of blows are also visible on the nose and upper lip. The mustache and mouth are twisted slightly to the right, presumably because the cloth was not evenly applied to the face. On the whole, however, the face, as seen in the negative, is reproduced with very little distortion.

Streaks of blood are noticeable on the forehead and in the hair. One such streak is traceable to a sharp puncture, which is faithfully reproduced. Similar streaks of blood appear on the neck of the dorsal image (see Plate 16).

The shoulders and neck of the body have left no trace on the frontal imprint, suggesting that the head was bent forward and held in position by rigor mortis. The contours of the chest and stomach appear clearly, as do the forearms and hands, which are crossed over the groin, obscuring the genital region (see Plate 11). The delicacy of the shading allows the observer to distinguish each finger, but on both hands the thumbs are obviously missing. As we shall see later on, the missing thumbs are of the utmost importance in determining the authenticity of the Shroud.

On the left side of the rib cage, a heavy stain thought to represent a gaping wound appears (see Plate 14). From this wound there was a copious flow of abnormally thick blood, such as might issue from a corpse. A clear, organic fluid also ran from this wound, and it has left a faint stain that extends beyond the edges of the blood flow.

On the right wrist, there is a heavy bloodstain, obviously caused by a major wound. A trickle of blood runs from the wound up the right forearm. The left wrist is obscured by the right hand, which overlaps it, but there is a similar trickle of blood running up the left forearm, indicating a wound on the left wrist, as well.

On the dorsal image, the back, buttocks and thighs are covered with streaks of blood that fall into a roughly regular pattern (see Plate 17). The blood appears to have clotted over excoriations such as might have been caused by severe scourging. In many cases, the wounds inflicted by the bits of bone or lead lodged in the thongs of Roman whips can be seen quite clearly. Traces of severe abrasions also appear in the region of the shoulders (see Plate 16).

The direction of the blood flow in most cases suggests that the body was in an upright position when wounded and for some time thereafter. The blood from the wrist wounds indicates that the arms were extended and bent at two different angles, as would be the case with a man hanging from a cross, alternately lifting himself up and letting himself hang (see Plate 10).

Dr. Robert Bucklin, a forensic pathologist and longtime student of the Shroud, presently chief medical examiner for Travis County, Austin, Texas, describes the feet:

> On the Shroud there are two prints representing the marks left by blood-covered feet. One of these, the mark of the right foot, is a nearly complete footprint on which the imprint of the heel and the toes can be seen clearly. In the center of this is a square image surrounded by a pale halo and representing the position of the nail in the foot. The imprint made by the left foot is considerably less clear and does not in any way resemble a footprint. Examination of the calves of the legs on the dorsal view shows that the right calf has left a well-defined imprint on which the marks of the scourge can be seen clearly. The imprint of the left calf is considerably less distinct, and this, coupled with the fact that the left heel is elevated above the right heel, leads to the conclusion that there is some degree of flexion of the left leg at the knee, and that the development of rigor mortis has left the leg in this position. It appears that the right foot was directly against the wood of the cross and that the left leg was flexed slightly at the knee, and the foot rotated so that the left foot rested on the instep of the right foot. By this position, the blood on the soles is easily accounted for. A single nail was then used to fix both feet in position.

In various places on the body imprints of the Shroud, stains appear to result from small drops of serous fluid that exuded from the pores of the body; such serum flows from a corpse.

There is no trace anywhere on the Shroud of putrefaction, indicating that the body must have been removed from the Shroud before decomposition began to damage the cloth.

In later chapters we will explore exactly how this mysterious two-thousand-year-old "photograph," with its medically accurate physical properties, could have come to be. But it is first necessary to clearly establish the known history of the Shroud and to deal with the archaeological questions of its origin.

III

The Testament of the Gospels

Writing in the *New Catholic Encyclopedia*, the Reverend Adam J. Otterbein, a Redemptorist priest and president of the Holy Shroud Guild of Esopus, New York, states, "If the Shroud of Turin is authentic, the imprints of the body must concur with the details of the Gospel account of the Passion." This attitude has influenced virtually every reasonable historical study of the Shroud, pro or con, that has been conducted, and immense exegetical effort has gone into establishing or refuting such corroboration.

There is, in fact, a substantial case for arguing that the origin of the Shroud and its markings do not violate Gospel descriptions, as we shall see. But we must accept the fact that the Gospels *as we know them* are controversial in both form and content, regardless of their original veracity and historical accuracy, and regardless of our own religious beliefs. Of dubious authorship, corrupted by copyists, possibly with parts missing and others out of place, misinterpreted in translation, perhaps censored, lacking in critical detail and presenting disparities among themselves, the Gospels are at best incomplete records of the origin of Christianity generally and of the Shroud specifically. Nonetheless, they are the only records we have, and they must therefore be carefully studied. But where there are, or seem to be, conflicts between the texts of the Gospels and the authenticity of the Shroud, then neither can take precedence over the other without considerable additional evidence.

Because of their similarities in content, chronology of events and manner of expression, the first three Gospels—those attributed to the evangelists Matthew, Mark and Luke, and dated between A.D. 40 and 100—are commonly referred to as the Synoptics. As such, they present a reasonably unified account of the Passion.

For the purposes of this book, I shall recount only those parts that have relevance to the Shroud, paraphrasing from the translation of The New English Bible. Points of particular importance are italicized for emphasis.

On Friday morning following Jesus' "trial," when Pontius Pilate had finally concluded that nothing short of Jesus' death would satisfy the chief priests and elders, *he had Jesus flogged and handed him over to be crucified.* Pilate's soldiers stripped Jesus and dressed him in a scarlet (or purple) mantle. *A crown of thorns was placed on his head,* and a cane in his right hand. He was jeered, spat upon and *beaten about the head with the cane.* When the soldiers had finished their mockery and abuse, the mantle was removed and Jesus was again dressed in his own clothes. Then he was led away to be crucified. *On the way, Simon of Cyrene was pressed into service to carry the cross.*

Arriving at Golgotha, the place of crucifixion, *Jesus was "fastened" to the cross* (or *"was cruci-*

fied"), and was further abused. The hour of crucifixion was nine o'clock in the morning. From mid-
day until about three in the afternoon, a darkness
fell over the whole land. At about three o'clock,
Jesus cried out, and a bystander offered him a
sponge soaked with sour wine, which he held to
Jesus' lips at the end of a cane (or short javelin).
Jesus again gave a loud cry, and died.

It was the day before the Sabbath, and when
evening came, Joseph of Arimathaea, a wealthy
disciple, approached Pilate and requested the body
of Jesus. Pilate was surprised that Jesus was already dead, but after establishing that fact, he
decreed that Joseph should have the body. *Joseph
took the body down from the cross, wrapped it in a
clean linen cloth which he had bought, and placed
it in his own unused tomb, which had been cut
out of rock.* He then rolled a large stone against
the entrance and left. Mary of Magdala and Mary,
the mother of James and Joseph, were watching
and saw where Jesus was laid.

On Saturday, the Sabbath, the chief priests and
Pharisees asked Pilate to place a guard on the
tomb so that Jesus' disciples could not steal the
body away and then claim he had risen from the
dead as he had prophesied. The tomb was sealed
and a guard was left in charge.

*Early on Sunday morning, after the Sabbath
was over, a group of women went to the tomb
with spices, oils and perfumes in order to anoint
Jesus' body.* When they arrived, they found that
the stone had been rolled away and Jesus was
gone.

Although somewhat vague and sketchy, nothing
more than an outline really, that is the essence of

events as revealed in the Synoptics. As we explore
them detail for detail, we will see that they present no significant obstacle to the authenticity of
the Shroud. But first we must examine the Gospel
of John. Again, important points are italicized.

Of the four Gospels, that of John is generally
considered the most controversial and also the
most troublesome where the Shroud is concerned,
although it does contain some important details
not mentioned in the Synoptics. Reputed to have
been written by the Galilean fisherman who was
one of the earliest and most devoted disciples,
the Fourth Gospel differs in many respects from
the Synoptics. Because of the numerous discrepan-
cies, there is considerable doubt that John the
Apostle was actually the author. That question,
however, is a matter for other books. Our task is
to determine the relationship between the text,
whoever the author, and the Shroud.

Where the Synoptics merely say that Pilate's
soldiers beat Jesus about the head, John is more
specific, recounting that they *struck him on the
face.*

John's description of the time of crucifixion
would seem to make it somewhat later than the
hour fixed by the Synoptics, since, according to
John, Pilate did not send Jesus away to be crucified until noon.

John specifically says that *Jesus carried his own
cross.*

To the account of the Synoptics, John adds the
important detail that the Friday of the crucifixion
was not only the eve of the Sabbath, but of Passover as well.

Following Jesus' death, John describes the blow

with the lance, which is not mentioned by the Synoptics:

Because it was the eve of Passover, the Jews were anxious that the bodies should not remain on the cross for the coming Sabbath, since that Sabbath was a day of great solemnity; so they requested Pilate to have the legs broken [to hasten death] and the bodies taken down. The soldiers accordingly came to the first of his fellow victims and to the second, and broke their legs; but when they came to Jesus, they found that he was already dead, so they did not break his legs. *But one of the soldiers stabbed his side with a lance, and at once there was a flow of blood and water.*

John's description of the burial is as follows:

After that, Pilate was approached by Joseph of Arimathaea, a disciple of Jesus, but a secret disciple for fear of the Jews, who asked to be allowed to remove the body of Jesus. Pilate gave the permission; so Joseph came and took the body away. He was joined by Nicodemus . . . who brought with him *a mixture of myrrh and aloes, more than half a hundredweight. They took the body of Jesus and wrapped it, with the spices, in strips of linen cloth according to Jewish burial customs.* Now at the place where he had been crucified there was a garden, and in the garden a new tomb, not yet used for burial. *There, because the tomb was near at hand and it was the eve of the Jewish Sabbath, they laid Jesus.*

Here is John's account of the events of Sunday morning:

Early on the Sunday morning, while it was still dark, Mary of Magdala came to the tomb. She saw that the stone had been moved away from the entrance, and ran to Simon Peter and the other disciple, the one whom Jesus loved. "They have taken the Lord out of his tomb," she cried, "and we do not know where they have laid him." So Peter and the other set out and made their way to the tomb. They were running side by side. but the other disciple outran Peter and reached the tomb first. *He peered in and saw the linen wrappings lying there,* but did not enter. Then Simon Peter came up, following him, and he went into the tomb. *He saw the linen wrappings lying, and the napkin which had been over his head. not lying with the wrappings but rolled together in a place by itself.* Then the disciple who had reached the tomb first went in too, and he saw and believed: until then they had not understood the Scriptures, which showed that he must rise from the dead.

Later on Sunday, in the evening, eleven of the disciples were together in a room when Jesus came to them. *He showed them "his hands and his side."* The twelfth disciple, Thomas, was not present, and when the others told him they had seen Jesus, he did not believe them.

He said, "Unless I see the mark of the nails on his hands, unless I put my finger into the

place where the nails were, and my hand
into his side, I will not believe it."

A week later his disciples were again in the
room, and Thomas was with them. Although
the doors were locked, Jesus came and stood
among them, saying, "Peace be with you!"
*Then he said to Thomas, "Reach your finger
here; see my hands. Reach your hand here
and put it into my side.* Be unbelieving no
longer, but believe." Thomas said, "My Lord
and my God!" Jesus said, "Because you have
seen me you have found faith. Happy are
they who never saw me and yet have found
faith."

(Of the Synoptics, only Luke mentions this episode, and then only vaguely; John's account is
much more detailed.)

Using the four Gospel accounts as the framework for our analysis, we must now compare
them, point by point, with the images and markings on the Shroud, supplementing our knowledge
with historical information not detailed in the
Gospels.

THE FLOGGING

According to Matthew (27:26), Mark (15:15)
and John (19:12), Jesus was severely scourged,
or flogged, at the praetorium before setting out for
Golgotha. In Luke (27:18, 23), Pilate twice attempted to have Jesus let off with the flogging as
his only punishment, but Luke does not specifically say that the flogging took place.

Markings on the Shroud reveal copious flogging

wounds, at least one hundred, perhaps even more. Shaped like tiny barbells, the contusions cover the entire image of the body, from the shoulders to the lower part of the legs, most of them appearing on the dorsal image (see Plate 18).

In addition to having been a general punishment in and of itself, flogging seems to have been a customary accompaniment to any execution, regardless of the final method of death—usually crucifixion, impalement or beheading. Prior to execution, the victim was stripped, his hands were tied in front of him to an upright stake or column and he was whipped from behind. Sometimes he was also whipped on his way to the place of execution. Jewish law forbade administering more than forty lashes, and the Pharisees had reduced the number to thirty-nine. Among the Romans no such restraint, short of death, is known to have been applied. We can be certain that many died, though perhaps not immediately, from either infection or internal hemorrhaging. The Shroud indicates that Jesus was struck excessively.

The Gospels describe the scourging with the technical term *flagellare*—"to whip." From the details of the wounds as seen on the Shroud, it is quite clear that Jesus was flogged with the *flagellum,* or, more likely, with the larger and heavier *flagrum* (see Plate 19). These dread instruments of punishment consisted of short handles to which several long thongs or chains were attached. Near the striking ends of the thongs, bits of bone or lumps of lead were affixed, their sole purpose to bite deeply into the flesh of the naked victim, weakening him and reducing his resistance to the ordeal to come.

The *flagrum* was a brutal device, so abhorrent that it was not used on Roman citizens or, generally, on free men. For them, the law reserved the *virga*, the rod or switch. But Jesus was treated as an outcast and criminal of the lowest order. And once Pilate had ceremoniously washed his hands of the whole affair, it is no great wonder that the best Jesus was to receive was the worst that the Romans could conceive.

THE CROWN OF THORNS

One of the most extensive studies of crucifixion and its attendant circumstances was undertaken by the Reverend U. Holzmeister, and published in 1934 in *Verbum Domini*, the review of the Pontifical Biblical Institute, under the title "Crux Domini eiusque crucifixio ex archaeologia romana illustrantur." Holzmeister believed that ridicule was obligatory to a Roman crucifixion, and that the crown of thorns—along with the dressing of Jesus in fine garments, the placing of the cane in his hand and the verbal mockery—was an example of this.

Unfortunately, Holzmeister's fragmentary sources do not conclusively prove his case, and it is difficult to believe that such elaborate proceedings were the rule of the day. Regardless of the excesses we might wish to attribute to the Romans, crucifixions were just too common for such elaborate displays to have taken place with all but the most exceptional victims. At any rate, the crown of thorns, as far as can be determined, was a unique feature of the crucifixion of Jesus.

Matthew (27:29), Mark (15:18) and John (19:2) attest that the crowning actually took place—"Plaiting a crown of thorns they placed it on his head." Luke is silent on the subject.

On both the frontal and dorsal images of the Shroud, what appear to be droplets of blood encircle the head. And because of additional bloodstains higher on the scalp, some medical authorities believe that the crown of thorns was not the circlet or wreath-shaped headband so frequently depicted in Christian art, but rather was shaped like a cap or helmet and covered the entire head, with plaited rushes securing it under the chin (see Plate 9). Thorns said to have come from the crown exist throughout the world and have been venerated by Christians for centuries. Although impossible to authenticate, they belong to a type of lotebush common in Judea. They are long and sharp—quite capable of having produced the abundant flow of blood which appears on the Shroud.

THE BEATING ABOUT JESUS' HEAD

All four Gospels are in accord that Jesus underwent several series of beatings prior to crucifixion (Matthew 26:67–68, 27:31; Mark 14:65, 15:19; Luke 22:63–64; John 19:3). Fists and a cane or stick were used, and the blows were aimed specifically at his head or face.

Medical authorities, most notably Dr. Pierre Barbet, have noted that the markings on the Shroud show a large bruise on the right cheek, as well as evidence indicating that Jesus' nose was broken.

CRUCIFIXION

The origins of crucifixion and the extent to which it was used as a means of execution in antiquity are unclear. Most authorities believe that the Persians practiced crucifixion regularly; but this assertion is based on the testimony of Greek authors, Herodotus in particular, and the practices of the Persians are referred to with verbs (*anastauroun* and *anaskolopzein*) that could easily refer to impalement on a pointed stake rather than crucifixion. Darius I of Persia (521– 486 B.C.), speaking in the Behistun inscription of the execution of his enemies, used an expression that is usually translated as "I impaled." Impalement was common in the ancient Near East, particularly among the Assyrians, who depicted it in their triumphal reliefs.

It is often said that the Greeks before Alexander the Great recoiled from crucifixion, but Herodotus states that during the Persian Wars (490–479 B.C.), Greeks crucified Artayctes, the Persian governor of Sestos. In describing the event, Herodotus does not use the suspect verbs mentioned above. On the contrary, his language is prophetic of things to come: "They nailed him alive to a plank. . . . Having nailed him to a plank, they hung him up."

There is little doubt that crucifixion was widely practiced in the Hellenistic monarchies of the Near East, by the Phoenicians, and in Carthage. Among the Romans, crucifixion, as we understand it, seems to have been introduced at the time of the Punic Wars in the third century B.C., and was thought of as a punishment primarily for slaves. A master had absolute power over his slaves, and severe punishment could be, and was, meted out for the most trivial of reasons. Punishment was administered with special rigor, and by the state, in the case of slaves who revolted. When the slave insurrection led by Spartacus was quelled in 71 B.C., six thousand crosses lined the road from Capua to Rome.

Pirates, bandits and rebellious subjects of the Roman Empire were also punished with crucifixion. Vivid examples of the latter category are recorded in Judea. The legate Quintilius Varus, having put down a rebellion which followed the death of Herod the Great in the year 3 B.C., crucified two thousand rebel leaders. During the siege of Jerusalem in A.D. 69, those who were caught trying to escape from the city were crucified in full sight of its walls. The executions often exceeded five hundred per day, and it is said that the soldiers amused themselves by varying the positions in which the condemned were attached to their crosses.

The crucifixion of Roman citizens, however, was regarded as an outrage. In 201 B.C., Scipio Africanus crucified the Roman deserters handed over to him by the Carthaginians, and both Livy and Valerius Maximus record the horror over this act. Cicero's catalogue of the atrocities committed by Verres, the Roman governor of Sicily, culminates in the description of the unjust and cruel punishments inflicted by him, and this mass of horrors is crowned by a dramatic account of the crucifixion of a man who claimed to be a Roman citizen.

Crucifixion seems to have been regarded as the most painful and the most ignominious form of capital punishment. The practice was discontinued by Constantine, the first Christian emperor, in about A.D. 314.

THE CROSS

The Roman cross consisted of two parts: an upright stake fixed in the ground (*palus, stipes*), and a transverse beam (*patibulum*). The stake always stood outside the city walls; in Rome, a whole forest of crosses stood outside the Esquiline gate.

Some Shroud scholars have debated whether the cross of Jesus was high off the ground or low. There are numerous references to the devouring of the bodies of the crucified by wild beasts, so it appears that many crosses were low. At least one cross in Roman history was a high one, as is clear from an anecdote in Suetonius' *Life of Galba:* When a man who had been condemned to the cross protested that he was a Roman citizen, Galba, the Roman emperor in A.D. 69, ordered that a high and whitewashed cross be prepared for him.

The Gospels do not refer to the size of the cross on which Jesus was mounted, but they do say that as he was hanging a sponge was held up to his lips at the end of a cane or stick (Matthew 27:48; Mark 15:26) or on the point of a javelin (John 19:29).

It seems useless to argue on the basis of the Gospel passages that the cross was either high or low. Certainly something would have been used to pass the sponge to Jesus in either case. Those present at the crucifixion were not strangers to the phenomenon. They knew what the ordeal

did to a man, and no one in his senses would bring
his hands near the mouth of a man in the grip of
severe convulsions for fear of having his fingers
bitten.

The external evidence suggests that the cross
was usually low, and there is nothing in the Gospels to indicate that the cross of Jesus was exceptional. The point is significant to the Shroud only
as it concerns the location and direction of the
lance thrust in the side. Although medical authorities disagree, it is extremely doubtful that the
evidence will ever be conclusive.

The controversy, no matter how slight, does
help to point out the complexities of dealing with
the Shroud, particularly in light of the fragmentary and often contradictory textual and archaeological evidence with which we must deal.

Some crosses were equipped with a projecting
peg (*sedile*), which was straddled by the condemned man. This is mentioned only by late, but
pre-Constantinian, authors Justin and Tertullian,
who refer specifically to the crucifixion of Jesus.
Though the peg is not shown specifically in Christian art, the omission seems to be a matter of
reverence rather than concern for literal fact.

At some time and with some crucifixions, the
footrest, or *suppedaneum*, might also have been
appended to the cross. The earliest mention of this
is in the Middle Ages, although some authorities
have discerned a footrest in the third-century Pal-
atine graffito, a satirical wall-drawing mocking a
Christian named Alexamenos.

The *sedile* and *suppedaneum* would have supported the crucified man, thus reducing the weight
on the nails through the wrists and prolonging his
suffering. Origen wrote that the crucified often

lived through the night and the following day, and Eusebius contended that the victims of the cross died of hunger. Neither statement can be true of all crucifixions, but they can be taken as indications that agony was often prolonged. The fact that Pilate was surprised when told that Jesus had died after only a few hours on the cross might indicate that some sort of support was common and was used on Jesus' cross. But that argument is weak, indeed.

The condemned were sometimes tied with rope to their crosses, but it was more customary to nail them. In Greek, to "nail up" means to crucify. Nails were driven through the victim's wrists and feet, although it is a matter of some controversy whether the feet were secured together with one nail or separately. The most compelling evidence, based on medical examinations of the Shroud and on a recent archaeological find, is in favor of the one nail.

Of the crucifixion itself, the Gospels say only that Jesus was "fastened" to the cross (Matthew 27:35; Mark 15:24) or that he "was crucified" (Luke 23:33; John 19:18). There are no details. Yet, if anything at all is certain about the Shroud, it is that the man represented on it was crucified with nails through his wrists and feet (see Plate 7). The wounds are there for all to see. They are startling in their reality, and there can be no confusion as to what they represent.

THE CARRYING OF THE CROSS

When the Greeks spoke of "carrying a cross," they undoubtedly meant carrying a part of the

cross—namely, the *patibulum,* or crossbeam. Latin sources mention only the *patibulum.* The procedure is alluded to, but not clearly described, in Jesus' prophetic words to Peter (John 21:18-19):
"'. . . when you were young you fastened your belt about you and walked where you chose; but when you are old, you will stretch out your arms, and a stranger will bind you fast and carry you where you have no wish to go.' He said this to indicate the manner of death [crucifixion] by which Peter was to glorify God."

Most of the extant references to the fact that condemned men were forced to carry their own crosses concern slaves. A slave, naked and bearing his *patibulum,* was whipped while walking through the most public places of the city on his way to execution. The *patibulum* was placed across his shoulders, and his wrists were tied to its extremities, although Dionysius of Halicarnassus speaks of a beam laid across the chest and shoulders of the condemned man.

Of Jesus, we are told that he "took up his own cross" (John 19:17), and also that it was carried for him by Simon of Cyrene (Matthew 27:32; Mark 15:21; Luke 23:26). The Gospels are again silent on details, but here we can at least make some reasonable assumptions in piecing together the story and reconciling the Gospel accounts. Jesus probably did begin carrying the crossbeam —estimated to have weighed about eighty pounds —as was customary, but owing to his weakened condition from the flogging and beatings and to the ruggedness of the terrain, he fell frequently. His movement toward Golgotha, a distance of approximately six hundred yards, was exceptionally slow and tedious. Because of the approaching

Passover Sabbath, everyone wanted the crucifixion to be completed as soon as possible, and thus Simon was enlisted to carry the crossbeam the remainder of the way.

In an effort to verify this contention, Monsignor Giulio Ricci, a Vatican archivist who has spent almost three decades studying the complexities of the Shroud, attempted, with the help of a hired man, to duplicate the walk of Christ. Unlike Jesus, the man was fit and healthy, but in simulating the journey he fell so many times that the experiment had to be stopped before they reached Golgotha.

On the Shroud, a mass of tiny lacerations across the image of the right shoulder indicates that a rough, heavy object chafed the shoulder. The object was almost certainly a crossbeam. Wounds on other parts of the body give evidence of numerous falls along a rocky path.

The Blow with the Lance

Of the Gospels, John (19:31–37) alone refers to the important detail of the lance thrust. Because the Jews did not want the bodies of Jesus and his two companions to remain on their crosses during the Passover Sabbath, they asked Pilate to have their legs broken and the bodies removed from the crosses.

The Latin term for this breaking of the shins following crucifixion is *crurifragium*. Its purpose was exactly opposite that of the *sedile* and the *suppedaneum*. While the latter were specifically designed to prolong the victim's life and agony on the cross, the *crurifragium* would assure a rapid death by bringing on tetany and asphyxia.

From the references of Seneca, Ammianus Marcellinus, Origen and Plautus, we can be reasonably certain that *crurifragium* was a common practice in and around Rome. But Jesus was already dead, so there was no need for his legs to be broken. Instead, one of the soldiers pierced his side with a lance. Why?

Usually the victims of crucifixion were left on their crosses to be devoured by wild beasts or birds of prey or to rot. According to a Roman law of the imperial period, however, it was possible for the families of the deceased to obtain the bodies for decent burial. In such cases, a single reference of antiquity suggests that the executioners were required by law to administer a sort of *coup de grâce* to the crucified—even when they were apparently already dead—before giving over the remains to the mourners. Quintilian, an author of the first century, writes: "Crosses [or the crucified] are cut down, and the executioner does not forbid the burial of those who have been smitten [or pierced, presumably with a sword or javelin]."

Origen, in the Latin translation of his *Commentary on Matthew*, says that the lance thrust was administered "according to Roman custom, below the armpit." Such a blow would correspond exactly with the location of the wound in the side as seen on the Shroud (see Plate 14). That wound resembles an elongated oval and is 1¾ inches by ⁷⁄₁₆ of an inch. These dimensions suggest that an incision made by the *lancea* commonly used by Roman auxiliaries—a spear with a long, leaflike tip that rounded off toward the shaft. From the wound of the lance, a massive flow of blood is evident on the Shroud—a large, dark stain intermingled with smaller, clear stains— the "water" described by John.

THE SHROUD AND THE BURIAL

So far there have been no significant conflicts between the markings on the Shroud and the relevant Gospel passages. Neither the Shroud nor the Gospels violate the archaeological framework, scant though it is, into which they must be placed. If we had only the Synoptics with which to contend, such would be the case throughout the remainder of this discussion. But as we arrive at the two most crucial points of the Gospel narratives—their specific references to the Shroud and their accounts of the actual disposition of Christ's body—John's text presents problems.

In the Old Testament, burial was regarded as a matter of the utmost importance. One was expected to bury even strangers and enemies, and failure to do so was considered a sign of great wickedness. Bodies were either interred in graves dug into the ground or placed in tombs hollowed out of rock. Rock tombs generally had shelves or troughs in the shape of coffins along the walls. This is suggested in the Old Testament and confirmed by archaeological evidence found in Palestine.

There is every reason to believe that burial took place as soon as possible after death, preferably on the same day. Even corpses of criminals who had been suspended from trees were taken down before sunset and buried. It was, and still is, customary in the Middle East to bury as quickly as possible because of the rapid decomposition of bodies in the extreme heat. The Jews considered a dead body polluting to the touch.

In the Old Testament, Jacob and Joseph, as important personages in Egypt, were mummified in the Egyptian manner. Embalming or other preparations for the tomb are not otherwise mentioned in the Old Testament, and archaeology has revealed no mummies in Palestine. According to the Mishnah, the body of Jewish law first codified by Rabbi Judah in about A.D. 200, a body was washed and anointed as the first step of burial. Present-day custom suggests that perhaps the washing was done with warm, perfumed water, though there is no evidence in the literature. Neither is there any indication of what ointments were used or exactly how the anointing was performed.

In the Old Testament, the mighty were buried with the garments, ornaments and weapons that had belonged to them in life. By the time the Mishnah was compiled, many considered obligatory a raiment so sumptuous that dying people were often abandoned by their relatives, thus leaving the trouble and expense of the funeral to the community at large. This abuse was rebuked by the examples set by Rabbis Gamaliel and Judah, who bade their heirs inter them in simple linen sheets. Linen garments were generally spoken of in connection with the funerals of the humble.

The eyes of the corpse had to be shut. The chin of the deceased was held in place by a chinband, and although nothing is said in the rabbinical literature of tying the hands and feet with thongs or bands, it may be safely assumed that this practical necessity was also common. Only in the Mishnah do we hear of the covering of the face with a handkerchief. It is stated that this had formerly been the practice of the poor, whose faces had been made unsightly by their privations, but the rule later became generalized. Here, as elsewhere in the Mishnah, it is difficult to apply a time-frame to the information given, but it is safe to assume that the practice was extant at the time of Jesus' death. Whatever garments were worn to the tomb, and however they were arranged, the face of the deceased was not generally concealed by them. Even the most ascetic rabbis who were buried in simple sheets probably wore the sheets draped around their bodies, as they had done in life. Whether in splendor or in simplicity, Jews were buried in clothing rather than in shrouds. The handkerchief over the face was at first optional and later mandatory, but the main garment was never draped over the head.

Thus, if Jesus did receive the complete and customary ritual burial, the Shroud of Turin could not possibly be the true burial cloth, for there are two absolute imperatives to the Shroud's authenticity in that respect: First, the burial cloth of Christ must have been a large, single sheet of linen that was wrapped lengthwise around the body, from head to foot. It could not have been arranged like a garment. Second, the burial must have been provisional and temporary rather than complete. If it had been complete, and the body thus washed and anointed according to custom, there would have been little, if any, blood left on the body to be transferred by direct contact onto the Shroud.

Let us now, once again, pick up the Gospel chronology. The Synoptics (Matthew 27:57–61; Mark 15:42–47; Luke 23:50–56) are in agree-

ment concerning the key elements of what happened: Joseph of Arimathaea petitioned Pilate
for Christ's body so that it might be buried. Receiving permission after some delay, Joseph
wrapped the body in a clean linen sheet (Mark
says he bought it specifically for the purpose), and
laid it in a new, unused tomb that was cut out of
rock (Matthew says it was Joseph's own tomb).
Mary of Magdala and Mary, the mother of James
and Joseph, followed him and saw where and how
Jesus was entombed.

(To have played such an unusual and important
part in the story of Christ, Joseph of Arimathaea
is a shadowy figure about whom little is known.
Undoubtedly he was a rich Jew, probably a member of the Sanhedrin, the highest religious and
secular council of his people. A secret disciple, he
had attempted to protect Jesus from his fate before boldly declaring his faith following the crucifixion. It is ironic, if not apocryphal, that the man
who was responsible for providing the Shroud is
also credited—by medieval legend—with carrying
the Holy Grail to England in about A.D. 64, and
founding the first Christian church in that country.)

The ancient Greek word used by the Synoptics
for the burial cloth is *sindon*, which means precisely a sheet of linen. *Sindon* can also be used
generally to designate a single strip of linen used
for any purpose: a sheet, a garment, a sail, and
so forth. Its modern Greek descendant, *sendoni*,
means bedsheet. It is from *sindon* that the word
for study of the Shroud—sindonology—is derived.

Several non-biblical texts use *sindon* in a funerary context, referring to it as the outer wrapping of a mummy. In its only other occurrence in the New Testament (Mark 14:51), it describes a garment, a sheet draped around the body like a robe. It also appears with the same meaning in a recently revealed paragraph that either was interpolated into Mark's Gospel after it was written, or, as some believe, was originally written by Mark and later suppressed. In that paragraph, brought to light by the controversial *Clement of Alexandria and a Secret Gospel of Mark* by Morton Smith, a young man was initiated into the mysteries of the kingdom of God in an all-night ceremony wearing nothing but a sindon.

The Synoptics' use of the word *sindon* is thus clear and accurate, with no ambiguities: Jesus was wrapped or enfolded in a large, single sheet of linen. The Shroud of Turin is a large, single sheet of linen.

Regarding the burial, the Synoptics are equally clear: Joseph wrapped the body in the linen sheet and laid it in a tomb cut out of rock. That is all they say about it. There is no mention of the body being washed. There is no mention of its being anointed. There are no details to support a complete ritual burial.

We *are* told that Mary of Magdala and Mary, the mother of James and Joseph, were watching and saw where and how Jesus was laid. *After* they saw this, they bought and prepared spices, oils and perfumes, either early Friday evening (Luke 23:55, 56) or after sunset on Saturday (Mark 16:1). They rested on the Sabbath. But very early on Sunday morning, the two Marys and probably other women returned to the tomb, bringing with them the unguents they had pre-

pared, *intending to anoint the remains* (Matthew
28:1; Mark 16:1; Luke 24:1). If the burial,
which they had seen, had been complete, there
would have been no reason for the women to
purchase and prepare the unguents or to return
to the tomb with the specific intent of anointing
the body.

Thus, the Synoptics at least circumstantially
support a temporary, provisional burial, with Jesus
wrapped in a large, single linen sheet.

John supports the Synoptics in stressing the
late hour and the haste with which the burial was
performed because of the approaching Sabbath
(John 19:31). According to his account, however, not everything was done by Joseph; Nicodemus appeared on the scene, bringing with him
a mixture of myrrh and aloes. The quantity of
this mixture is a matter of scholarly debate, but
it was undoubtedly considerable—between fifty
and one hundred pounds. It is believed to have
been in powdered or granular form, and its singular importance would have been to serve as a dis-
infectant, arresting the process of putrefaction.

Joseph and Nicodemus then "took the body of
Jesus and wrapped it, with the spices, in strips
of linen cloth, according to Jewish burial customs"
(John 19:38–42).

The New English Bible translation of the above
passage is open to many objections. "According
to Jewish burial customs" is too free. A word-for-
word translation of the Greek text gives us: "as
is the custom of the Jews in laying out a body."
Entaphiazo, the Greek verb used, can only mean
"lay out"; if "bury" had been intended, then the
proper verb would have been *thapto*. Thus, John

does not say that a definitive burial took place. What Joseph and Nicodemus did undoubtedly was in accord with custom, but nowhere is it said that they performed every ministration obligatory to the completion of the ritual. Every reasonable indication is that they did not.

The verb translated "to wrap" (*deo*) means "to tie, to bind." It cannot really apply to the swathing with small strips of cloth, as suggested by The New English Bible. It cannot apply at all to wrapping in a large, single sheet. There is, however, a variant reading of some authority in the early Greek manuscripts that is supported by early Syriac translations. The verb used in these is *enilesan* (from *eneileo*), the same verb that Mark uses to describe the wrapping of the body in the sheet. It is a much more appropriate verb for the application of either a sheet or strips of cloth, so it is quite difficult to understand why a copyist would replace it with the problematic *deo*.

John says the body was wrapped in "strips of linen cloth"—*othonia*. *Othonion* (singular) means much the same as *sindon*—a piece of linen in any of its applications. In the plural, as used by John, the word can only designate more than one linen cloth. How, then, can this word be reconciled with the single sheet referred to in the Synoptics or with the Shroud of Turin? There are several theories:

1. The sheet mentioned by the Synoptics was, there and then, torn into strips, thus becoming the "cloths" observed by John. This solution, said to go back to Salmasius, does reconcile with the Synoptics, but it destroys the authenticity of the Shroud. In addition, there is absolutely no evi-

dence to support the assumption that bands or bandages swathed the corpses of Jews, either as a general custom or under special circumstances. And whatever the cloth or cloths used, John is quite explicit that custom was observed.

2. *Othonia* means a variety of cloths, not many cloths of the same size and shape. This, too, is an old solution, revived with fresh force by A. Vaccari, a Shroud scholar who points to a papyrus inventory of the personal effects of an agent of the Roman government who made a trip from upper Egypt to Antioch in about A.D. 320. In the listing, under the general heading of *"Othonia"* are grouped a variety of linens, including four *sindones* and two kinds of handkerchiefs (*fakeria*). If we accept this theory, then John's references to the *othonia* could designate the large sheet of linen singled out by the Synoptics, plus all the smaller cloths or bands that would have been necessary to effect even a provisional burial.

This theory is far more acceptable than the first, since it was almost obligatory that such a variety of cloths—in addition to the *sindon*—be used in the disposition of Jesus' body, even temporarily. Binding the jaw of a corpse is common, even today. The tying of the hands and the feet was a practicality, necessary to counteract the forces of rigor mortis and make it easier to transport the body to and into the tomb. In addition, such bindings would allow a more dignified way of laying out the body.

The verb *deo* still eludes our understanding, for while it could be appropriate in referring to the binding of the hands, feet and jaw, its usage is incorrect in reference to the application of the *sindon,* for which the textual variant *eneileo* ("wrap") is better.

3. According to the last theory, *othonia* refers only to the linen bands that were used to secure the hands, feet and, possibly, the jaw. In *The Shroud of Turin,* Werner Bulst, former professor of fundamental theology in the Jesuit theological seminary at Frankfurt am Main, claims a measure of originality for this idea, which alone explains the use of the verb *deo.*

If *deo* is, in fact, precisely the expression that John intended, then the Bulst theory is sound. It is certainly supported by John's description of the raising of Lazarus (John 11:44). There, John specifically mentions the binding of the hands and feet, using the verb *deo,* which is perfectly in context. And there, too, John omits any mention of the large cloth that Lazarus most surely wore in the tomb and continued to wear as he emerged (although the *sindon* of Lazarus, because he had received a complete, ritual burial, would have been worn as a garment, in death as in life).

But why does John completely ignore the *sindon,* to which his fellow evangelists unanimously attest? There is not now and probably never will be an acceptable answer.

Moving forward in John's text, on Sunday morning Mary of Magdala made her way to the tomb for an unspecified purpose. Seeing that the stone had been removed, she ran to tell Peter that the body had been stolen. Peter and another disciple (John himself, it is widely believed) hurried to the tomb. The latter arrived first and stopped at the door. He saw the *othonia* "lying there." Peter then entered the tomb and saw not merely the *othonia,* but also "the *sudarium* that had been over Jesus' head, not lying with the *othonia* but folded [or rolled] in a place by itself. Then the disciple who had reached the tomb first went in too, and he saw and believed; until then they had not understood the Scriptures, which showed that he must rise from the dead." (John 20:1–9)

(In some editions of the Bible, Peter's discovery of the linen cloths is also mentioned in Luke [24:12], where the word *othonia* is used. Some New Testament scholars believe the passage to be an interpolation from John, but a growing number of people, including the Right Reverend Dr. John A. T. Robinson, Anglican dean of chapel and lecturer in theology at Trinity College, Cambridge, believe that it is part of Luke's original text. The passage is omitted in only one Greek manuscript. If the passage is indeed Luke's, then it circumstantially supports the theory that the *othonia* included the *sindon* that Luke had earlier mentioned.)

The *sudarium* to which John refers is a new term, a new piece of cloth not mentioned before. It means handkerchief or napkin (literally "sweat cloth"), and no other meaning is attributed to it in either Greek or Latin, from which the Greeks took the word.

In the case of Jesus, the *sudarium* could be a thin, porous veil used to cover the face in death. As such, its use would neither affect the authenticity of the Shroud nor be prohibited by Jewish burial custom, although the exact historical period when such face veils were used is a matter of some ambiguity. Whether such use can be reconciled with John's choice of words—"the *sudarium* which was *over* his head," not over or covering his *face*—is again subject to debate.

If a *sudarium* (a handkerchief or sweat cloth) could be over fourteen feet long and over three feet wide, then it could be the Shroud itself. But, as Dr. Robinson has pointed out:

> The only reason for supposing, as some have, that the *sudarium* was itself the Shroud, is that the latter clearly did go over the head and face, as well, of course, as the whole body. Yet, neither in the case of Lazarus [John 11:44] nor in that of Jesus does [John] say that the *sudarium* covered the face. We are told [in the original Greek] that it was "round the face of [Lazarus]" and "over the head" of [Jesus].
>
> The only position, I submit, that fits both these descriptions, assuming they are referring to the same custom, is that of something tied crossways over the head, round the face and under the chin. In other words, it describes a jawband, which would have been required to keep the mouth shut and, together with the closing of the eyes, would have been functionally necessary before rigor mortis set in.

To form the jawband or chinband from the *sudarium*, the almost-square handkerchief would have been folded (or rolled) diagonally, wrapped under the chin, brought vertically around the face and tied over the head.

This explanation conforms perfectly to what John says Peter saw upon entering the tomb. It provides a description of the obligatory chinband in even a provisional burial and can be reasonably reconciled with John's choice of words. It is also in harmony with the visual evidence of the Shroud. Bulst, Robinson and other observers have noted that the imprints of the locks of hair down the cheeks are strong, as if bunched forward by the chinband. The beard, on the other hand, seems to have been retracted under the chin. Also, the vertical strips (dark on the negative photograph, light on the Shroud) on both sides of the face, between the cheeks and the locks, could have been caused by the band holding back, and thus hiding, the intervening hair. If the chinband were tied over the top of the head, this could explain the pinched or bunched effect at the top of the head and also provide a partial answer to the question of why no image appears where the crown of the head should have been positioned against the Shroud (also fully explained if the Shroud were lying loose and not pulled tightly around the crown of the head).

It is thus possible, though problematic, to explain the cloths John saw applied to Jesus' body, and later left in the tomb, without denying the authenticity of the Shroud. Yet, although numerous scholars and exegetes have tried, there is simply no way that the problems introduced by John's choice of words (or the corruption thereof by copyists of the original and subsequent texts) can be completely resolved on the basis of existing documents. But, as perplexing as these problems are, they are essentially issues of linguistic interpretation rather than historical fact. And in light of the scientific evidence for the Shroud's authenticity, they seem minor, indeed.

In no other way does the Shroud or its markings conflict with the Gospels, with other historical sources or with our present archaeological knowledge.

IV

The Lost Millennium

In historical terms, the Shroud of Turin can be
traced back with certainty to 1356, but its appearance in Lirey, France, in that year remains un-
explained. Its owners deliberately obfuscated the
question of its origin, and its exposition gave rise
to accusations and scandals which provide the
substance of the principal arguments of opponents
of the Shroud's authenticity. Another focal argument against it is the striking lack of references
to the relic from the time of Christ and the Gospels
until 1356. Only one text, which refers to the year
1204, mentions a shroud possessing the unique
qualities of the Shroud of Turin. Overzealous
proponents of the Shroud's legitimacy have, to be
sure, adduced many other texts, but these have
served only to fire the incredulity of those capable
of understanding their wording and context.

The astonishing historical silence which surrounds the Shroud begins with the Gospels themselves, for only John says cloths were found in
the tomb, and he says nothing of the most striking
feature of the Shroud of Turin, namely, the images
of the body. Nonetheless, the burial cloth of Christ
certainly occupied the imagination of early Christians. It is often mentioned in the apocryphal
Gospels, and in one of them, the Gospel According

to the Hebrews, it is mentioned that after the resurrection, Jesus gave the Shroud "to the servant of the priest," or "to Simon Peter," the latter being the interpretation of some scholars who believe the text is corrupt. This Gospel, preserved only in fragments, enjoyed the esteem of the fathers of the church, many of whom thought it to be the original version of the Gospel of Matthew.

Early Christian apologists pointed to the finding of the cloths in the tomb as proof of the resurrection. If the body had been stolen, they asked, would it not have been easier to carry it in its shroud? There is no indication, however, that these writers knew any more about the Shroud than what they had read in the Gospels. Another early school of thought within the church held that the cloth spread over the altar for the sacrament of Holy Communion was the symbol of the Shroud.

Saint Nino, who brought Christianity to Georgia during the reign of Constantine the Great (A.D. 306–337), is said to have meditated much on the Shroud as a girl in Jerusalem. When she asked her teacher, Niaphori, "the most learned Christian in Jerusalem," about it, she was told that nothing was known, but that tradition affirmed it had been kept by Saint Peter.

Also during the time of Constantine, Eusebius of Caesarea, sometimes known as the father of ecclesiastical history, wrote to Constantia, the emperor's sister, that a portrait of Christ was an impossibility, since only God knew his spiritual nature, while his physical appearance was forever lost. Eusebius frowned on all pictures and statues which purported to show the actual likeness of Jesus, for such representations were the objects

of excessive veneration and, to him, smacked of
heathen practices. Still later, Saint Augustine
wrote that the representations of Christ were in-
numerable, "although his appearance, whatever it
was, can only have been one."

The first mention of an existent Shroud appears
in an account of the Holy Land written in about
570 by a pilgrim from Piacenza. The anonymous
chronicler. who lent a ready ear to the tall tales of
guides and solemnly reproduced them in his work,
reports that the Shroud was said to be preserved
in a cave convent by the Jordan. He himself had
not seen it, however.

About a century later, Arculph, a French bishop,
made a pilgrimage to the Holy Land. On the return voyage, bad weather forced him to put in at
Iona, off the coast of Scotland, where the details
of his eventful journey were recorded by the Bene-
dictine abbot Adamnan. Among the marvels of
Jerusalem was "the shroud which covered Jesus'
head in the tomb." It was exposed for veneration
every other day, and Arculph saw, venerated and
kissed it.

A legend attached to the object on display in
Jerusalem, also duly reported by Arculph, said
that it had been stolen after the resurrection by
a converted Jew, and that its possession enriched
him vastly. When he lay dying, he offered his two
sons the choice between all his worldly possessions
and the Shroud. The son who chose the possessions promptly squandered them; the one who
chose the Shroud was soon as wealthy as his
father had been. The Shroud remained in the same
family down to the fifth generation, but then it fell
into the hands of infidel Jews, who also grew rich
from their possession of it. The existence and

properties of the Shroud became common knowledge in Jerusalem, and the Christians grew vociferous in claiming it for themselves. The dispute was submitted for judgment to an Arab ruler, who took the Shroud and placed it, with his own hands, in a burning fire. The cloth was not damaged and, before long, it rose from the fire, hovered in the air, and finally fell to earth near the Christian spectators. The Christians glorified God and placed the relic in a church.

Arculph described the Shroud he saw as being about eight feet long, and mentioned neither bloodstains nor images. But if the cloth he saw was the Shroud of Turin, he could hardly have avoided seeing them; and any rationalizations to the contrary are just not acceptable. Nonetheless, Arculph's account has been discussed in almost every study of the Shroud, and some sindonologists have taken great pains to explain away the problematic eight feet: one school believing that the Shroud was folded for display, another that Arculph did indeed see the entire length but referred to it in terms of the ancient Piedmont foot. The latter, translated into contemporary measurement, would make the shroud Arculph saw equal 13.482 feet, not significantly less than the 14 feet, 3 inches of the Shroud of Turin, and Arculph did qualify his measurement with "about."

All of this is at best an example of the academic pettifoggery that has impaired serious consideration of the Shroud since its discovery. Arculph's account, as well as a number of others which will not be repeated here, proves only one thing: the burial cloth of Christ—existent or not, witnessed or not, one and the same as the Shroud of Turin or not—was an important symbol of

the Christian faith, as were any number of other
relics, real or simulated. It should be noted here
that in medieval Europe there were at least forty-
three "True Shrouds," both plain and figured,
some of them obvious copies of the Shroud of
Turin. As only one example of the extreme naïveté
with which they were accepted, the famous Shroud
of Cadouin was discovered—in 1935—to be a
Moslem cloth embroidered with texts praising
Allah. Thus, all of the ancient, uncorroborated
testaments to the existence of the Shroud must be
treated with the utmost skepticism.

From about the year 1000 onward, a shroud is
mentioned in catalogues of the relics preserved
at the imperial court in Constantinople. Again,
nothing is said of marks or stains, let alone a dis-
cernible image. In 1201 Nicholas Mesarites,
patriarch of Constantinople and head of the Eastern church, examined and described those precious
relics. The funeral cloths of Christ, he says, "are
of linen, of cheap material, such as was available.
They still smell of perfume; they have defied decay because they enveloped the ineffable, naked,
myrrh-covered corpse after the Passion." If Mesarites saw images, he did not mention them, but
some scholars have deduced from his citing of the
"naked" body that he knew more than he told,
since the concept of a naked Christ, in any circumstances, has not been favorably looked upon
throughout the history of Christianity, but is immediately evident on the Shroud.

Finally, in 1204 Robert de Clari, a chronicler
of the Fourth Crusade, wrote that before the fall
of Constantinople to the Crusaders, a shroud was

exhibited every Friday at the church of Saint Mary of the Blachernae, and that on this shroud the figure of Christ was clearly visible. "After the city was taken," he added, "no one, neither Greek nor Frenchman, ever knew what became of it." Since de Clari himself arrived with the Crusaders, however, it would seem that he did not see the relic with his own eyes.

Relics did count as important booty in the sack of Constantinople. Large numbers of venerable objects were sent to Europe, and it was not long before more relics than Constantinople ever had were in circulation. Cloths advertised as parts of the Holy Shroud found their way almost at once to towns in France and Germany. One "part" remained in Constantinople only to be presented in 1247, along with other relics, to Louis IX of France. Parts of that part were in turn exchanged by the king for other relics. It is possible, though I believe improbable, that the strip of linen sewn along the entire length of the Shroud replaced the portion that Louis IX possessed.

Perhaps the object described by Robert de Clari was indeed the Shroud of Turin, but if so, no light has ever been shed upon the 152 years that elapsed between its disappearance from Constantinople and its appearance at Lirey.

The documented historical case for the authenticity of the Shroud is exceptionally poor and only slightly improved by attempts to explain the silence of historical sources.

To the Jews, it has been argued, anything that touched a corpse was impure; to the Gentiles, crucifixion was the most ignominious of punishments, and it was unthinkable that a god in human form—a familiar idea in the Greco-Roman world —would submit to it. The Shroud had touched what was, at one point, a corpse, and bore chillingly graphic witness to a crucifixion. Under these circumstances, the custodians of the Shroud, whoever they were, could not have been eager to display the controversial artifact.

The idea of Jesus crucified was so repellent to early Christians that it significantly affected not only the spread of the new religion, but also the artistic tradition that arose from it. There was almost a tacit law that forbade pictorial representations of the crucifixion, and this would have imposed even greater restraint on public expositions of the Shroud, so stark was the reality of its depiction.

The earliest pictures of Jesus show him as a clean-shaven youth. He appears as a fisherman, a shepherd, a teacher, as the leader of a dance, but not in any of the degrading phases of the Passion. The cross became, almost at once, the symbol of the new religion; but the earliest artistic representations of the crucifixion date only from the fifth century. One of these crucifixion scenes, on a wooden panel of the door of Santa Sabina in Rome, is also one of the earliest works of art in which Jesus is shown bearded. Crucifixion scenes became a little more common in the sixth and seventh centuries, but as late as 692, an ecclesiastical council at Constantinople found it necessary to ordain that the figure of Christ be depicted on the cross, and not merely symbolized by a star or a lamb.

The politics of the church continued to discourage speculation about the Shroud. In 725, a tendency of eastern Christianity came strongly to the fore: the use of icons or devotional images was condemned, and the imperial dynasty led the struggle to suppress such pictures and relics. The controversy lasted, with interruptions, until 845. The iconoclasts, or opponents of the images, would have had little use for the Shroud, but the iconodules, or picture-venerators, would have had every reason to preserve it, perhaps in hiding. If the iconodules did know of the Shroud, however, there are no references to it, and it is astonishing that they would make no mention of it in their polemical writings, particularly in light of their citing of another image of Christ's face on a cloth as a sign of divine approval of these images. And after the final defeat of iconoclasm in 845, there can have been no reason to conceal the existence of the Shroud and every reason to see that it received the widest possible display. But again there is only silence.

Thus, with the exception of Robert de Clari's all-too-vague account of the disappearance of a figured shroud from Constantinople in 1204, there are no reliable reports to substantiate the existence of the Shroud of Turin prior to 1356. Certainly none of the references to Holy Shrouds or burial cloths can be said to designate anything with the unusual properties of the Shroud as we know it. This disconcerting lack of pedigree has given much ammunition to critics, and at the same time it has moved some proponents into almost absurd rationalizations for the millennium's silence.

Now we must ask: Is it possible the Shroud did

exist, and has a documented history, but was thought to be something entirely different from what it is? It is with these questions in mind that we must consider the Holy Image of Edessa.

V

The Holy Image of Edessa

Edessa (now Urfa, in southern Turkey) was a Syrian border town and early center of Christianity, which was probably introduced there sometime in the second century A.D. During the Persian siege of that city in 544, a cloth was found inside a wall over the city gate. On it there was what was believed to be a miraculous image of Christ. This cloth, generally referred to as the Holy Image of Edessa or the Edessan Image, is the most important of several such pictures or images of Christ that began to turn up in the sixth century and were said to be *acheiropoieton*—"not made with hands."

In searching for a history of the Shroud in the millennium following the crucifixion, we find little of significance except this mysterious Edessan Image. Could it be possible, then, that these two images of Christ are intrinsically related? If authentic, the Shroud of Turin has its origin at the crucifixion. Apart from its remarkable discovery in the wall in 544, the origin of the Edessan Image is unknown.

There is, of course, the standard and seemingly obligatory progression of legends. According to Eusebius, who based his tale on documents he claimed existed in the Edessan archives, Abgar V, king of Edessa from A.D. 13 to 50, was ill and became interested in new religions. Thus, he sent an envoy to Jesus, asking him to visit the Edessan court. Jesus declined but sent a letter promising good things for Abgar and his people.

The mid-fourth-century *Doctrine of Addai* states that Abgar's envoy, Ananias, painted a portrait of Jesus and took it back to Edessa. Eusebius (writing in about 320) mentions no image in his account, but given his aforementioned animosity toward depictions of Christ, the omission would not have been out of character. The source of the two reports seems to be one and the same. The eminent British historian of the Eastern church, Sir Steven Runciman, notes that Eusebius "included the passages placed immediately before and after the portrait episode in the account given in the *Doctrine*," making his suppression of the detail all the more conspicuous. The Abgar/Jesus correspondence, based on studies of quotations from it, was unquestionably bogus, since it contained phrases copied directly from the Gospels and included theological dictates of a time following the death of Jesus.

In about 730, John of Damascus, the foremost opponent of iconoclasm, wrote that the Edessan Image originated when Ananias was unable to paint a satisfactory portrait of Jesus. Thus, Jesus obligingly picked up the cloth and pressed it to his face, thereby imprinting it with a miraculous likeness of himself. John wrote in such dogmatic terms that not even the iconoclasts dared dispute him. That his testament to this tradition was self-serving is obvious, but it does mesh with the extraordinary reverence accorded the Image.

Having virtually no factual basis that we can

now document, these stories and the widespread dissemination of them seem nothing more than attempts, eminently successful at the time, to provide an acceptable provenance for the perplexing cloth that most certainly did exist, and which, in the words of the Reverend Maurus Green, a British priest and historian, "acquired an artistic, theological and political importance far greater than any other icon before or since."

Although Runciman never associated the Edessan Image with the Shroud, he did chide historians who had dismissed the significance of the Image because of its murky origins, and he rightly stressed its importance in history, saying, "This dim piece of canvas [did] exercise a direct influence on the destinies of Christendom."

Among its lesser influences, the Edessan Image and the tradition of its miraculous origin were almost certainly the root sources for the legends of "Veronica's Veil" and their corresponding depictions of the face of Jesus (supposedly miraculous, but, in fact, painted), all of which were predated by the Image and its legends. In medieval times, these figured cloths were referred to as "veronicas," a popular corruption of the words *vera icon* ("true image").

During the siege of Edessa by the Persians in 544, the newly found Image was paraded around the barricaded city, miraculously aiding in the repulsion of the attackers, or so it was believed.

By the time of the iconoclast controversy (725–845), Edessa was no longer part of the Byzantine Empire, and not only was the Image safe from the fury of the iconoclasts, but it also became one of the most powerful weapons in the defeat of their argument. Runciman wrote in 1931:

"Indeed to the less subtle it offered an argument for unqualified image worship; and as a concrete proof that Christ disagreed with the iconoclastic theories it provided the sort of refutation that carried the most weight in the Middle Ages."

The fame of the Edessan Image became so widespread and its authority so widely heralded that the Byzantines had to have it. Father Green writes:

Once Iconoclasm was finally defeated in 845, Orthodox Constantinople could not long remain without possession of its most powerful weapon. In 943, the old emperor, Romanus Lecapenus, sent his army to invade Syria with special instructions to obtain the Image. Edessa was besieged. The city would be spared, if the Image was handed over in exchange for two hundred Moslem hostages. After long negotiations and unsuccessful attempts by the citizens to pass off two copies as the real thing, the Byzantine army returned in triumph in 944. The Image, by now known as the *Mandylion*, was given the welcome reserved to conquering generals. It was taken with great piety round the city walls, in through the Golden Gates to Santa Sophia, to be lodged finally in the imperial Chapel of the Bucoleon. Christ himself had entered his own city. Henceforth he would guard it against all attacks, as he had once guarded Edessa. On occasion his Image was carried round the walls as a defense measure, when the city was under siege.

Until the crusaders ravaged Constantinople in 1204, the Edessan Image ranked as a treasured relic. After that date its fate is unclear, and after that same date, the figured cloth referred to by Robert de Clari as the Shroud also disappeared . . . from the same city, possibly from the same resting place. Were the two actually only one? And was the Edessan Image what we now know as the Shroud of Turin?

British historian Ian Wilson, who has spent a decade studying this aspect of the Shroud's existence, believes the two are, in fact, one. He commissioned the first complete translation of *Narratio de Imagine Edessena,* an "official" history of the Edessan Image written by a member of the court of the tenth-century emperor Constantine Porphyrogenitus. The history gives a description of how the Image appeared to the Byzantines: "a moist secretion, without any coloring or artificial aid." It is a rather strange description of something that might be considered a painted icon, but it is an almost perfect description of the image visible on the Shroud of Turin.

The work also mentions the viewing of the Image in 944 by Constantine Porphyrogenitus and his brothers-in-law. Constantine saw the portrait clearly, but to the others it seemed "extremely blurred." (Lest I be accused of forcing a comparison with the Shroud Image here, it must be acknowledged that all of the young men were notorious drunks, and it might well have been their vision that was "extremely blurred.")

The history adds yet another legend to those of the Image's origin: the likeness became visible after Jesus wiped the bloody sweat from his face with the cloth in Gethsemane. If the Shroud and the Edessan Image are one and the same, this revisionist addition might well have been an attempt to explain the recognizable bloodstains on the cloth without admitting that Christ was crucified, an untenable admission at the time of the history's origin.

One of the problems Wilson faces in linking the Edessan Image with the Shroud of Turin is that the dominant tradition of the Edessan Image maintains that only a face is visible, not the entire body. Wilson contends, however, that he has found evidence to support the thesis that whenever the Edessan Image was shown, it was "doubled in four." And folding the Shroud of Turin in exactly that way will produce the same "disembodied" head seen on copies of the Edessan Image. Evidence supporting this contention is found in the two groups of small, charred circles especially visible at the sides of the loins on the dorsal image of the Shroud. Another two groups occupy the same positions on the frontal image. The generally accepted notion is that the circles were caused by a fire prior to the one that damaged the Shroud in Chambéry. But the nearly uniform size of the circles, their regular spacing and their correspondent positioning when the Shroud is folded do not appear to be the result of an accident. Whatever their cause—Wilson presently leans in favor of some kind of ordeal or ritual that involved touching the cloth with a red-hot poker—they indicate that the cloth was folded when displayed.

Since Ian Wilson is preparing for publication his own manuscript on the Shroud, it would be unfair to reveal more of his thesis. There is, however, one other area of study that offers some support for the belief that the Edessan Image and the Shroud of Turin are one and the same: the many artistic reproductions of Christ's face that began to appear in the sixth century. This is referred to by sindonologists as the iconographic theory.

Certainly Jesus had been depicted before the sixth century, but during that century the traditional appearance of Christ—with a long, oval face, shoulder-length hair, mustache and beard (usually forked), long nose, deep-set, staring eyes and a pronounced, arched eyebrow—became the dominant artistic conception. These features are not inconsistent with those that can be discerned on the Shroud, and, in several instances, they evidence almost uncanny similarity.

In addition, many of these sixth-century portraits, particularly those painted on cloth and believed to be copies of the Edessan Image show stylized anomalies also visible on the Shroud: a bruise across the forehead; a three-sided square between the eyebrows with a "V" shape below it at the bridge of the nose; a line across the throat (caused on the Shroud by some ancient crease); and two or three wisps of hair on the forehead (which could be the artists' attempts to cope with the trickles of blood that flowed from the punctures inflicted by the crown of thorns).

Is it possible, then, that the Shroud served as a model for these depictions, but, for whatever reasons, was at the time known as the Edessan Image?

To put this iconographic thesis into context, and to explain an extremely complex set of premises as simply as possible, let us construct a speculative history of the Shroud/Image from the crucifixion until its presumed disappearance from Constantinople in 1204.

Following the crucifixion and resurrection,

Simon Peter or another disciple came into possession of the Shroud. If the images were then visible, he was aware that he held the most miraculous of all miracles—a self-portrait of the risen Savior. Even if the images had not yet formed on the linen (a theory ventured by some students of the Shroud), the cloth itself would have been deemed valuable, if only as a personal keepsake of the disciple. But in either case, the cloth was also bloody and had touched the corpse of a crucified man. Neither Jew nor Gentile, no matter how strong his dedication to Jesus would have felt comfortable having it in his possession. In addition, while such a graphic reminder of Jesus' sacrifice might have served as a powerful symbol of the burgeoning new religion, it would just as certainly have been sought out by opponents of the sect and destroyed.

Its owner, perceiving all this, carefully hid it away, either hoping to reclaim it himself in more propitious times, or, in effect, willing it to future Christians. After hiding it, he may have mentioned it to other Christians from time to time, thus adding some substance, albeit unverified, to the rumors and legends about its existence.

Its hiding place, the brick city wall of Edessa, was discovered in 544, and while its new owners did not know—or did not want others to know— exactly what it was, they did identify it as a miraculous portrait of Jesus. But this was a portrait of a naked, crucified, suffering Christ, and both the artistic conventions and general concept of Christ during this time studiously avoided such portrayals.

As the Reverend Edward A. Wuenschel has written:

Even after Constantine abolished crucifixion, and the cross was brought into the open as an honored symbol, it took about three centuries for Christian artists to abandon their reverential reticence, but it was Christ living and triumphant, clad in a robe of glory and wearing a royal crown, that they portrayed on the cross, not Christ in agony or in death. It was only in the eleventh century that they ventured to be more realistic. The complete realism of the crucifix which is so familiar to us now did not make its appearance till the thirteenth century, and it was developed principally in the West.

Now on the Shroud the effects of Christ's crucifixion are visible in all their stark reality, more vivid and more appalling than in any artistic work. And not only the crucifixion. There are also the marks of all the other humiliating tortures of the Passion and traces of the process which took place after death. It is reasonable, therefore, to suppose that the Shroud was kept more or less hidden for centuries and a prudent silence observed about the imprint. . . . Those who imagine that the guardians of the Shroud should have gone about waving it like a banner show little understanding of the Christian Orient.

So the real Shroud/Image was kept discreetly out of sight. The few high-ranking priests and members of royalty who did view it saw a cloth that was folded (and very likely framed) in such a way that the battered and bleeding body (as well as most of the cloth) was kept hidden and only the remarkable majesty of the face was revealed.

At the time the Shroud/Image was discovered, the church was combatting the heresy of the Monophysites, who denied the human nature of Christ. The evidence of the Shroud itself would have provided a clear illustration of the incarnation, but since it was considered too graphic to be shown, a competent copy, supported by the Edessan legend of its miraculous origin, was probably deemed sufficient to rout the heretics. The fifth and sixth centuries were not sophisticated times, and, as in the later iconoclastic controversy, just about any religious argument buttressed with authority could have gained support.

Thus did an artist copy the facial image, adhering to the details of Christ's countenance as witnessed on the cloth, but changing the misty negative image of the death mask into a more conventionally accepted portrait of the living Christ. The newly painted "Edessan Image"—the public having accepted the copy as the real thing —met with great success, and soon the popular demand for more copies representing the "true likeness" of Christ was such that selected artists were allowed or encouraged to make duplications. (There was, conveniently, another tradition supporting the copies: the Image could miraculously duplicate itself.) Whether they worked from the actual Shroud/Image or from the copy, these artists were scrupulous in their attention to detail, and even though the haziness of the Shroud's image must have made it exceptionally difficult to copy, the similarities between it and a number of the reproductions are striking.

The iconoclast controversy that raged from

725 to 845 gave additional reasons to keep the real Shroud/Image hidden and well protected, and even later, it is unlikely that many people were allowed to see it.

When the Byzantine Army came to appropriate the Shroud/Image in 943, the Edessans tried several times to pass off some of their better copies as the real thing. But the Byzantines knew exactly what they were after, and the Shroud/Image that entered Constantinople in 944 was undoubtedly the original. It remained there until the sacking of the city by members of the Fourth Crusade in 1204. During their plunder, the Crusaders took everything they could lay their hands on, and what they couldn't carry back to the West, they destroyed. Among the spoils was the Holy Shroud.

This history takes into account the known currents of the church, particularly as they affected attitudes toward the visual display of Christ's likeness; it expands upon the few facts that are known, and it depends heavily on the similarities between the artistic depictions of Christ that began to appear in the sixth century and the facial image that is evident on the Shroud of Turin. The most prominent of these artistic reproductions are those of the *mandylion* class, which were painted on cloth and almost certainly had their inspiration in the Edessan Image, whatever the Image really was.

But the history is speculative. It provides the Shroud with the continuous, if unproven, historical thread it so vitally needs, but it is open to challenge on a number of points. Sophisticated historians and art authorities find contradictions and inconsistencies, but both supporters and opponents have only fragments of knowledge, and in the end—unless Ian Wilson or others are able to add significantly to the facts of this period—it is unlikely that a completely acceptable history of the Shroud will be found.

VI

The Pilgrimage of the Shroud

If the Shroud of Turin has only a speculative history before 1356, it has an exceptionally stormy one thereafter. Sometime between 1353 and 1356, the Shroud mysteriously turned up in the possession of Geoffroy de Charny (*père*) in Lirey, France. The exact date cannot be pinpointed, but since de Charny was killed in 1356, that is the earliest date we can use with certainty.

Little is known of Geoffroy de Charny; nothing is known of how he acquired this mysterious possession. A rather obscure French knight of the period, and the lord of the district of Lirey, he served in 1337 under the Count of Eu in the wars of Guyenne and Languedoc. In 1345, he accompanied Humbert II, dauphin of Viennois, on a foray into infidel territory. In 1348, in an attempt to take Calais from the English by ruse, he was captured by the British, from whose clutches he was ransomed by the king of France for one thousand gold écus. In 1355, he was designated to carry the battle standard of the king, a signal honor. An authority on questions of chivalry, he wrote a book on the subject, and was the author as well of verses expressing a rather stern sense of morality.

A series of documents dated from 1343 to 1356

indicate that de Charny sponsored a church at Lirey, in the diocese of Troyes. The documents show that Philip VI (king of France, 1328–1350) amortized income for the pious foundation; that two popes—Clement VI and Innocent VI—approved the regulations of the new canonry and enriched it with indulgences; and that the bishop of Troyes, Henri de Poitiers, gave the undertaking his blessing.

In the past, some scholars have asserted that de Charny founded the church for the specific purpose of housing and displaying the "true Burial Sheet of Christ." There are absolutely no documents to support this assertion, and the details of the documents that do exist concerning the foundation of the church—none of which mention the Shroud in any context—further refute the claim.

The evidence that the Shroud was displayed at Lirey during the life of de Charny is based on two documents. The first is a letter written by Pierre d'Arcis, de Poitiers' successor as bishop of Troyes, dated 1389. The letter states that the Shroud had been exposed at Lirey thirty-four years previously, "or thereabouts," around 1355. The second document, a decree issued by (anti-)Pope Clement VII in 1390, mentions that the Shroud was "reverently placed" at Lirey by de Charny.

De Charny never divulged how, where or from whom he had obtained the Shroud, and he took his important secret to the grave. If, however, the Shroud had indeed been at Constantinople before its fall, at least a kernel of speculation is possible. According to the Reverend A. J. Otterbein in his *New Catholic Ency-*

clopedia article, "It was not unlikely that [the Shroud] was taken to France at the time when the fall of Constantinople to the Orientals was foreseen. Further, it is known that the Latin Emperor's prime minister, who had access to [the Shroud], returned to the West shortly before the fall of Constantinople. He was of the family of the wife of Geoffroy de Charny. . . ."

As likely as this hypothesis might seem, it still leaves the question of who had the Shroud from 1204 until 1353–1356. Another unsupported theory suggests that the Shroud was given to de Charny by King Philip VI. In either case, the question remains: If de Charny had the Shroud in his possession for any period of time before his death, why is the relic not mentioned in any of the documents or records of the church at Lirey?

Nothing more is heard of the Shroud until 1389. In that year, Geoffroy de Charny (*fils*) obtained from Pierre de Thury, cardinal of Saint Susan and legate of the pope to Charles VI (king of France, 1380–1422), permission to exhibit the Shroud at Lirey. In his decree of 1390, Clement VII refers to this as permission to exhibit "a semblance or representation of the sudarium of our Lord." Letters from Charles VI confirmed the permission.

No permission was sought from Pierre d'Arcis, then bishop of Troyes. It was not long, however, before the extravagant ceremonies which attended the Shroud at Lirey, and the vast crowds of pilgrims attracted by the miraculous relic, drew d'Arcis' attention and his wrath. Angered by the slight to his authority and by the number of pilgrims deserting Troyes in favor of the more sensational attraction of Lirey, d'Arcis convened a synod (an ecclesiastical council), at which he forbade the clergy of the diocese to speak of the Shroud, whether for good or evil. He rebuked the dean of Lirey for exceeding the authorization of the cardinal-legate, which permitted modest expositions only, and forbade him on pain of excommunication to show the Shroud in any way to anyone at all.

The clergy of Lirey retorted by appealing to the Holy See. While waiting for a reply, they continued to expose the Shroud with great ceremony and solemnity. The messenger dispatched by the canons to the papal court at Avignon returned with a document from Clement VII in which the permission issued by the cardinal-legate was confirmed. The pope, moreover, imposed "eternal silence" regarding the subject of the Holy Shroud on Pierre d'Arcis.

The bishop, far from falling silent, immediately complained to Charles VI, and on August 4, 1389, the king withdrew the permission to expose the Shroud that he had previously granted. Furthermore, Charles wrote to the bailiff of Troyes, Jean de Venderesse, instructing him to confiscate the Shroud in the name of the crown. The bailiff's visit to Lirey is commemorated in a memorandum drawn up and signed by him on August 15; a second memorandum of the same date includes details that had "unfortunately" been omitted from the first. At Lirey, the good bailiff was met with a bewildering mass of sophisms, with appeals to the authority of Geoffroy de Charny and of Clement VII, and finally with a flat refusal to surrender the Shroud.

Baffled by the obstinacy of the canons, unwilling to give up the fight, Pierre d'Arcis then composed and addressed to Clement VII the long letter which later critics of the Shroud seized upon as the principal historical justification for rejecting its authenticity.

The basic substance of the letter (which will be reproduced in the following chapter) follows: According to d'Arcis, the first exposition of the Shroud (which he describes as taking place in 1355, "or thereabouts") was undertaken without the authorization of the bishop of Troyes, Henri de Poitiers. Henri proceeded to conduct an investigation. A committee of theologians and other prudent men assured him that the Shroud at Lirey could not possibly be genuine, since the Gospels say nothing of any imprints on the Shroud found in the tomb. Further inquiries made by Henri showed that the Shroud possessed by the canons of Lirey was a forgery, and this finding was corroborated by "the artist who had painted it": to wit, that it was "the work of human skill and not miraculously wrought or bestowed." (We will deal fully with the implications of this charge later, but suffice it to say for now that no documents of the alleged de Poitiers investigation survive, and if they did exist at the time, d'Arcis did not even mention them.)

Pierre d'Arcis' letter went on to condemn in the roundest terms the avarice and cupidity of the canons of Lirey, which led them to expose the Shroud with greater ceremony than attended the Holy Eucharist, to put into circulation rumors that it was the True Shroud and that it performed miracles and to encourage among the faithful the notion that its authenticity was sanctioned by the Holy See. D'Arcis voiced his concern for the souls of the faithful and expressed his confidence that permission to expose it had been obtained from the legate and the pope only because of serious misrepresentations. He regarded himself as justified in ignoring the pope's injunction to eternal silence.

What d'Arcis' letter lacked in proof and substance, it amply made up in rhetoric, and it must have been persuasive. But neither had Geoffroy (*fils*) been idle. He had addressed to the pope a complaint about the measures taken by the bishop, the king and the bailiff.

On January 6, 1390, Clement VII, assailed on all sides by appeals, complaints and recriminations, issued no fewer than three bulls on the subject of the Shroud:

1. A general decree *ad futuram rei memoriam*: The exposition of the relic is permitted, but the ceremonies censured by the bishop are forbidden. The relic is to be shown in a discreet way, and during the exposition it must be proclaimed loudly and intelligibly that "it is not the True Shroud of Our Lord, but a painting or picture made in the semblance or representation of the shroud."

2. To Pierre d'Arcis: He is forbidden to oppose the exposition of the relic. provided that the exposition take place in the manner and under the conditions prescribed by the pope.

3. To the ecclesiastical judges of Langres, Autun and Châlons-sur-Marne: They are exhorted to make known to all, and to assure the implementation of, the dispositions of the pope with regard to the Shroud.

It is presumed that the pope's directives were carried out for some years without incident, for nothing more is heard of the Shroud until 1418. In that year, Humbert, Count de la Roche, issued a receipt to the canons of Lirey for the relics and church ornaments confided to his care for the duration of a period of war and unrest. Humbert had married Marguerite, the daughter of Geoffroy de Charny *(fils)*, and thereby became lord of Lirey. He died without returning the relics that had been placed in his care, including what was dutifully described as "the semblance or representation of the shroud of Our Lord."

When the canons of Lirey tried to recover their possessions from the widow Marguerite, they found it necessary to summon her before the judicial court of Dôle. On May 8, 1443, she was compelled by threat of endless legal complications to surrender to the canons the "several relics and ornaments" that had been entrusted to her husband. But the area of Lirey was, in Marguerite's opinion, still unsafe. She was quick to point out that she was not bound by the signature of her husband with regard to the Shroud, which she claimed had been taken in war by her grandfather and could therefore be regarded as her own property. She did, however, promise to return the Shroud after three years, and agreed to pay compensation—twelve francs per annum—for the resulting loss of alms to the canons.

Four years later, the canons summoned Marguerite before the ecclesiastical judge of Besançon. She appeared on July 18, 1447, only to voice afresh her apprehension at leaving the Shroud in a disturbed area. The canons, with exemplary patience, consented to an additional delay of two years, but raised their demand of yearly compensation to fifteen francs.

In 1449 Marguerite and the Shroud appeared in Hainaut (a medieval county in northern France, now territory divided by Belgium and France). According to the chronicler Zantifliet, she arrived at Chimay (a town in the Hainaut district) with "a piece of linen on which was admirably depicted the form of the body of Our Lord." Rumor proclaimed this to be the True Shroud of Christ, and the faithful came streaming from the surrounding provinces to venerate it. When the matter reached the attention of Jean de Heinsberg, bishop of Liège, he dispatched two professors of theology to look into it. In the course of their investigations they required Marguerite to produce the documents that authorized her to display the relic. She showed them three bulls of Clement VII and an authorization issued by Cardinal "Pierre de Luna" (presumably Pierre de Thury). Each of these documents, according to the chronicler—and he reproduced textually one of the Clementine bulls —stated explicitly that the relic in question was not the True Shroud of Christ.

At the expiration of the second extension that had been granted Marguerite for the return of the Shroud (October 28, 1449), she was not to be found in Burgundy. On November 6, she was represented before the provost of Troyes by her brother, Charles de Noyers. The canons pressed, once again, for the surrender of their treasure; Charles recognized their right to it, but again obtained an extension of three years. He promised, in Marguerite's name, to fortify Lirey, which she still regarded as an unsafe resting place for the Shroud. Once more, the payment of an annual sum was arranged, even though neither of the previous sums had ever been paid.

Marguerite and the Shroud next appear in Savoy, at the court of Duke Louis I. On March 22, 1452, by all accounts, she presented the Shroud to the duke, who placed it in the sacristy of the Sainte Chapelle at Chambéry, France. No document attests to this transaction; nor is it clarified by references in later documents. Neither is there mention of the Shroud in the document in which Louis enfeoffs to Marguerite the town and manor of Mirabel in 1453, nor in the document in which he presents her with the town and manor of Flumet in 1455, as compensation for Mirabel, which has in the meantime been taken from her.

It was some time before the canons of Lirey recognized the full extent of their misfortune, but when they did, they were no longer content with halfway measures. On May 30, 1457, the ecclesiastical judge of Besançon, after a pro forma exhortation to return the Shroud to its rightful owners, issued against Marguerite a writ of excommunication.

Communication did not lapse, however, between the canons and their patroness. Marguerite promised to pay a compensation of eight hundred gold ducats for the Shroud, and on January 19, 1458, she was summoned before the provost of Troyes to explain her failure to keep that promise. Once more, Charles de Noyers appeared in her place. Once more, promises were made, this time by Charles in his own name. The sum would be paid, and an additional payment of three hundred pounds would reimburse the canons for the expenses of justice. It was also agreed that the relevant papal bulls would be surrendered to the canons, who were anxious to be able to document their ownership of the Shroud. It was agreed that the excommunication of Marguerite would be suspended until the date fixed for payment—October 1, 1458—and that upon payment it would lapse altogether.

On October 7 of the following year Marguerite died, having paid not a penny of compensation and still under sentence of excommunication.

The canons, cheated of their due by Marguerite and Charles, next approached the duke of Savoy. In Paris on February 6, 1464, Louis I issued a document in which the history of the Shroud was resumed and the conditions under which Marguerite had "transferred" it to the House of Savoy were left discreetly vague. Recognizing the substantial loss and diminution of income suffered by the canons, the duke assigned to them in perpetuity an annual income of fifty gold francs, demanding in return that a mass be said every year for the Holy Spirit, and after the duke's decease, for the repose of his soul.

In the midst of all this, the canons had not forgotten Marguerite, upon whose memory they heaped reproofs, and from whose agent, Philibert Thibaut, they refused to lift the ban of excommunication. On May 23, 1465, the duke wrote to them from Paris, chiding them for their intransigent attitudes.

A petition of 1472 or 1482—the date is uncertain—was addressed by the canons of Lirey to the king of France. The story of the Shroud is once again related; yet this time the canons complain of the duke of Savoy's failure to honor his financial obligations. In the petition, the canons request that the king himself assign the revenues to them until such time as compensation for the loss of revenue from the Shroud can be obtained. A fragmentary order issued by King Louis XI to the bailiffs of Sens, Troyes and Chaumont does not make clear the result of the petition.

In 1473, the canons dispatched representatives to Duchess Yolande—regent for Philibert, the grandson of Louis I of Savoy—to claim eight years of arrears in the income promised them in 1464. The outcome of the embassy is unknown.

It is known, however, that the Shroud has remained under the ownership of the House of Savoy ever since. It reposed in the Sainte Chapelle of Chambéry until 1578, and the only incident of note during that period was the fire that destroyed the sacristy of that church on December 4, 1532. As the fire raged through the structure, the flames licked the silver casket in which the Shroud was folded. Risking death, two laymen—Filippo Lambert and Guglielmo Pussod—and two unidentified Franciscan priests rushed into the flaming church and rescued the Shroud. It did not, however, escape unharmed. Drops of molten silver from the casket had fallen on the linen and burned through its forty-eight folds.

In 1534 the damaged Shroud was taken to the monastery of Saint Clare, where the nuns applied the patches that still remain.

In 1578, Saint Charles Borromeo indicated his desire to make a pilgrimage to the Shroud. To spare the venerated saint the rigors of crossing the Alps, the duke of Savoy ordered the Shroud transferred to Turin, where, with the exception of a hiatus during the Second World War when it was removed to Monte Vergine for safekeeping, it has remained ever since.

As John Walsh points out, "The years of the relic's stay at Turin were relatively quiet ones, with its public showings very rare. At first it was displayed annually, but such frequent handling and exposure, it was feared, would damage it unnecessarily. The 1898 Exposition was only the sixth time that nineteenth-century eyes had looked upon it."

In 1900, Ulysse Chevalier, the twentieth century's most severe critic of the Shroud's authenticity, yet at the same time its most meticulous historian, wrote: "The history of the Shroud constitutes a protracted violation of the two virtues so often commended by our holy books, justice and truth." If truth had prevailed, perhaps many of the controversies surrounding the Shroud could have been avoided. Unfortunately, that was not to be, though one must observe that Canon Chevalier would not be the least of the offenders.

VII

The Historians Attack

The publication of Secondo Pia's photographs of 1898 caused a worldwide sensation. Millions of Christians who had previously never even heard of the Shroud now found themselves vitally concerned with it; there was much talk of a miracle. It was in this context that Canon Ulysse Chevalier entered the controversy.

Born in 1841, Chevalier had distinguished himself at an early age. Entering the priesthood at twenty-one, he soon accumulated honor upon honor until, in 1883, he published his *Répetoire des Sources historiques du moyen age,* an exhaustive study that compiled almost all of the sources for the history of the Middle Ages. One critic labeled Chevalier "the most learned man in France and perhaps in the entire world," and another called his book "the most extraordinarily documented work a single man could produce."

By the early 1900s, when he became concerned with the Shroud, Chevalier was professor of ecclesiastical history at the Catholic Faculties of Lyon, and one of the most formidable and respected historians in the world. In the context of the Catholic world, he was a liberal: his philosophy closely resembled that of the Bollandists, the Belgian society of Jesuit scholars to whom

Chevalier repeatedly appealed in arguing about
the Shroud, and whose approval of his position he
regarded as decisive. The Bollandists had occupied
themselves with church history for over two centuries. Their special interest was in the lives and
legends of the saints, but the background and
authenticity of relics were also subjects of their
inquiries. They were among the pioneers and
principal exponents of liberal Catholic scholarship, treading treacherous ground between Funda-
mentalist Catholics, to whom critical research
into legends smacked of subversion and impiety,
and rationalist historians, who dismissed the
literature and practices of piety as unimportant
and absurd. Like the Bollandists, Chevalier remained, to the end of the Shroud controversy,
eager to free the church of grotesque beliefs and
customs in order to make way for a more modern and more solid spiritual foundation. In that
context, it is no small wonder that he chose
the Shroud, and the veneration accorded it, as a
symbol of what he considered wrong with the
church.

In Chevalier's first article on the Shroud—"Le
Saint Suaire de Turin est-il l'original ou une
copie?" published in 1899—he drew attention to
the case against authenticity made some years
previously by Canon Charles Lalore (in *Revue
catholique du diocèse de Troyes,* March 9 and 16,
1877). Lalore had examined most of the documents relevant to the Shroud, and had been
content to summarize them. They proved that
the Shroud had been regarded as a fraud in the
fourteenth century, and to Lalore, this meant that
it was a fraud.

Chevalier merely transcribed, word for word,

the arguments made by Lalore, and rested his case upon them. But he made his personal attitude to the question perfectly clear. He wrote, "The church is not afraid of the light; and in this case it will be seen that the light cast by written documents is brighter than the marvels of electricity."

From 1899 to 1903, Chevalier would publish nearly a dozen dissertations on the Shroud, and while the last of these would embroil him in technical and scientific arguments, his basic case would always go back to the documents, of which he found and published nearly fifty.

But what of these documents? What do they really prove? Virtually nothing, as we shall see.

The basic document used by Chevalier, as well as by most of the other historical critics of the Shroud's authenticity, is the letter from Pierre d'Arcis to Clement VII, in which d'Arcis sought, for once and for all, to stop the exposition of the Shroud at Lirey.

The key statement in the letter is d'Arcis' confirmation of the investigation undertaken by his predecessor, Henri de Poitiers, which proved that the Shroud was a forgery. Here, in translation, is the relevant portion of d'Arcis' letter:

> The Lord Henry of Poitiers, of pious memory, then Bishop of Troyes, becoming aware of this, and urged by many prudent persons to take action, as indeed was his duty in the exercise of his ordinary jurisdiction, set himself earnestly to work to fathom the truth of this matter. For many theologians and other wise persons declared that this could not be the real shroud of our Lord, having the Savior's likeness thus imprinted upon it,

since the Holy Gospel made no mention of
any such imprint; while, if it had been true,
it was quite unlikely that the holy Evangelists
would have omitted to record it, or that the
fact should have remained hidden until the
present time. Eventually, after diligent inquiry and examination, he discovered the
fraud and how the said cloth had been cun-
ningly painted, the truth being attested by
the artist who had painted it; to wit, that it
was a work of human skill and not miraculously wrought or bestowed. Accordingly,
after taking mature counsel with wise
theologians and men of the law, seeing that
he neither ought nor could allow the matter
to pass, he began to institute formal proceedings against the said Dean and his ac-
complices in order to root out this false per-
suasion. They, seeing their wickedness discovered, hid away the said cloth so that
the Ordinary could not find it, and they kept
it hidden afterwards for thirty-four years or
thereabouts down to the present year [1389].

The remainder of d'Arcis' letter is little more
than a sustained, yet completely unsubstantiated,
attack on the motives of those who would exhibit
the Shroud. As Father Wuenschel wrote in the
Ecclesiastical Review in 1935:

Taken on its own merits, the memorial of
Pierre d'Arcis is untrustworthy, because it
was written in anger and betrays a strong
bias against de Charny and the Dean of
Lirey. [Clement VII] himself, in his rescript
to de Charny and in his final decree, declares

that Pierre d'Arcis was angry with his opponents for obtaining an indult to exhibit
the Shroud without his permission. He was
still more angry with them when they ignored
his command to withdraw the Shroud from
public veneration, and invoked the intervention of the king to prevent him from taking
action against them. And he was hurt and
humiliated when [Clement VII] upheld his
opponents and put him under silence in the
rescript to the layman de Charny, leaving
the outraged bishop to learn of this censure
from common report. Pierre d'Arcis' memorial is a violent outburst over his grievances
and a piece of special pleading in his own
defense. He is so intemperate in his
language, so bitter in his animus against
those whom he accuses, so reckless in imput-
ing to them the basest motives, that we cannot rely on his unsupported statement that
they were guilty of the meanest kind of
fraud.

Father Wuenschel's comments are generally accepted and echoed by most contemporary scholars
who favor the Shroud's authenticity. If the d'Arcis
letter had not been regarded as so important, we
might leave it at that, dismissing it as inconclusive
and one-sided evidence at best. But even if the
letter were a vicious, self-serving attack on d'Arcis'
enemies, might there not be some substance to his
charges?

If Henri de Poitiers conducted an investigation
of the Shroud, there is only the d'Arcis letter to
say so. Throughout the exchanges, d'Arcis never
produced a single piece of supportive evidence.

Certainly d'Arcis, as de Poitiers' successor, would
have had access to all records, and had they existed, he undoubtedly would have produced them.
Neither is there any record of the investigation
in the work of Nicholas Camuzat, the historian of
the diocese of Troyes. Had the investigation actually taken place. it is unlikely that it would have
escaped the historian's attention. Finally, neither
Canon Chevalier nor any of his fellow critics have
ever been able to unearth any documents to support d'Arcis' charges. Given Chevalier's uncon-
tested aptitude for bringing to light precisely such
documents, as well as the vengeance with which
he sought to refute the authenticity of the Shroud,
it is inconceivable that even the slightest fragment
of support for his cause would have eluded him.

According to Pierre d'Arcis, the exposition of
the Shroud which caused de Poitiers to take action
against the canons of Lirey would have taken place
in 1355, "or thereabouts." But on May 28 1356,
de Poitiers issued his confirmation of the establish-
ment of the church at Lirey, to which he gave his
unqualified and lavish blessings. That document
does exist, and in it not a word is said about the
Shroud, about the investigation or about any
other relic. Are we to believe, then, that a bishop
who had been at such loggerheads with local
church officials just the year before would issue
such a laudatory document?

Even if we accept the imprecision of d'Arcis'
"or thereabouts" dating, the possibility that de
Poitiers' alleged investigation took place in some
other year faces the same lack of documentation.
In addition, the scant evidence available indicates
that the good relations between de Poitiers and
the canons of Lirey were unbroken throughout

THE SACRED SHROUD

PLATE 1
The face of the man on the Shroud, as it is seen on a
photographic negative. The trickles of blood in the hair
and on the forehead are results of the crown of thorns.
Art experts have found on the face a number of physical
details and anomalies which are also present on early
icons believed to be copies of the Edessan Image.

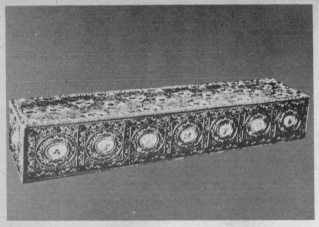

PLATE 2
The ornate silver casket in which the Shroud has been kept for centuries.

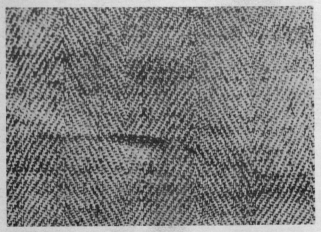

PLATE 3
An enlargement of the cloth from which the Shroud was woven. It is pure linen, a herringbone pattern woven in what is referred to as a three-to-one twill. Material of this type is believed to have been commonly available in Palestine during the time of Jesus.

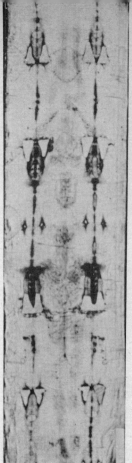

PLATE 4 (LEFT)
The full Shroud as it appears to the naked eye, with the frontal and dorsal images head to head. The dark lines which run the entire length of the Shroud, the triangular patches sewn on by the Poor Clares and the large, lozenge-shaped stains are the results of the Chambéry fire.

PLATE 5 (RIGHT)
The Shroud as it appears on a photographic negative. The continuous mistlike stains which comprise the body images have positive (or normal) characteristics of light and shade, while the bloodstains have negative characteristics.

PLATE 6
The frontal image as it appears on a photographic negative.

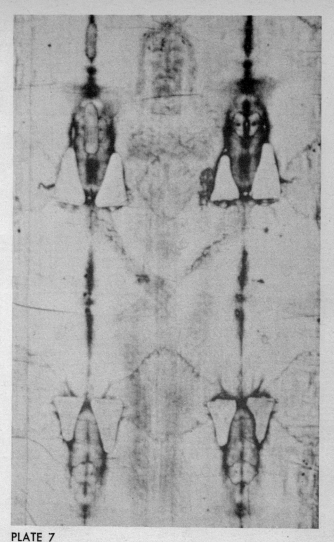

PLATE 7
The frontal image as it appears to the naked eye. Since the Shroud is itself a "negative," in the photographic sense, its colors and positions are reversed from the way they appear in reality.

PLATE 8

This sixteenth-century painting by the artist Giulio Clovio illustrates the manner in which the Shroud was wrapped lengthwise around the body of Jesus, allowing both the frontal and dorsal images to be reproduced on it. Although cropped in this photo, at the top of the painting are three angels displaying a crude reproduction of the Shroud, complete with its images and the markings left by the Chambéry fire of 1532.

PLATE 9
The images on the Shroud were used as the model for this sculpture of the crucifixion by Peter Weyland. The crown of thorns is more like a cap than the traditionally accepted circlet. As on the Shroud, the nails are pierced through the wrists rather than the palms; both feet are joined by one nail; and the expanded rib cage and contracted epigastric hollow point to death brought on by hanging from the arms.

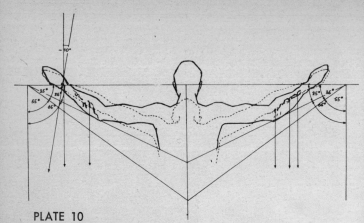

PLATE 10

This diagram illustrates Dr. Pierre Barbet's theory that the body of Jesus alternately lifted and sagged on the cross—the reason that the blood evident on the forearms flowed in different directions.

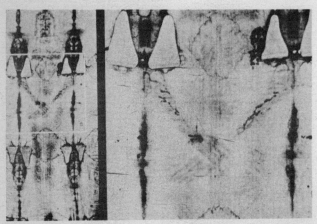

PLATE 11

An enlarged detail of the Shroud's frontal image. Note the wound in the wrist, the blood flows on the forearms and the large patch of blood which flowed from the wound in the side. Both thumbs are hidden from view, an anomaly explained by Dr. Barbet's experiments with cadavers.

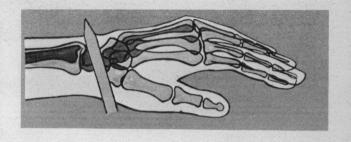

PLATE 12-PLATE 13 (BOTTOM)
These two X-ray-like diagrams show how the nail pierced the wrist of the man on the Shroud, according to Dr. Barbet's calculations.

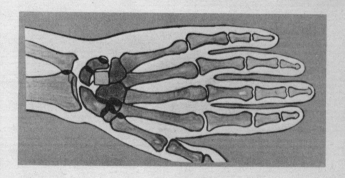

PLATE 14
An enlarged detail from the frontal image of the Shroud shows the large patch of blood and serous fluid that flowed from the wound in the side.

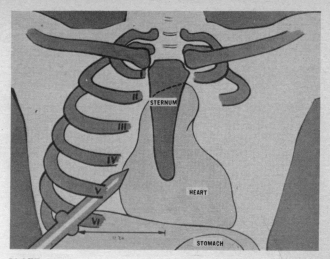

PLATE 15

This diagram illustrates Dr. Barbet's theory that the lance entered the body between the fifth and sixth ribs and then pierced the heart.

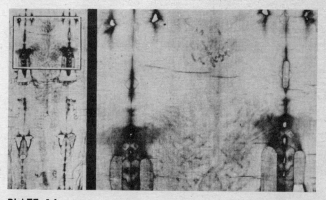

PLATE 16

An enlarged detail of the dorsal image shows the number of punctures inflicted by the crown of thorns and the excoriations that resulted from the chafing of the cross and the scourging.

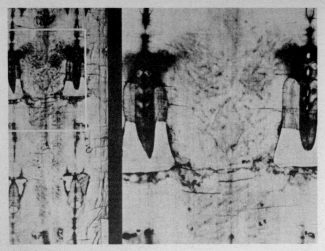

PLATE 17
An enlarged detail of the dorsal image shows the many scourge wounds. The transverse flow of blood across the lower back is believed to have issued from the heart when Jesus was being carried to the tomb in a horizontal position.

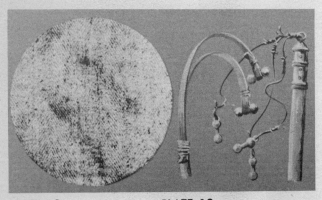

PLATE 18
An enlargement of the dumbbell-shaped wounds inflicted by the *flagrum*.

PLATE 19
Reproductions of the Roman *flagrum* used to scourge those marked for execution.

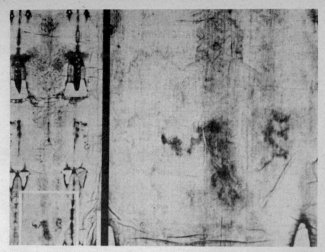

PLATE 20
This enlarged detail of the dorsal image shows the somewhat hazy area of the feet. They are turned inward, indicating that one nail was used to affix both feet to the cross.

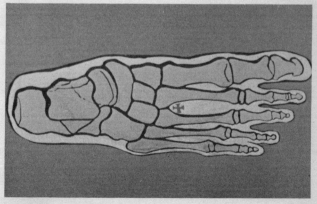

PLATE 21
The "X" in this diagram indicates the position of the nail that joined the feet to the cross.

PLATE 22
The Shroud on display at the Cathedral of Turin during the
exposition of 1933.

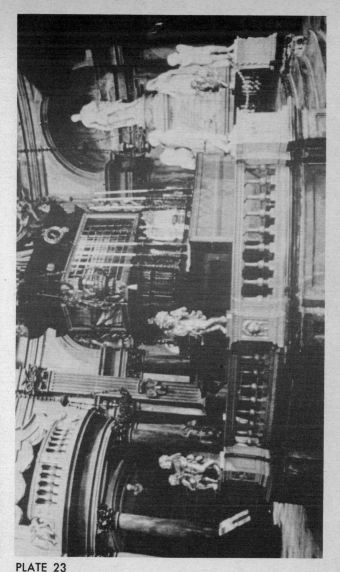

PLATE 23
The Royal Chapel of the Cathedral of Saint John the Baptist in Turin, Italy. The Shroud has been kept in a vault on the altar here since 1578.

PLATE 24-PLATE 25
Computer-reconstituted photographs of the Shroud and
the facial detail showing that three-dimensional qualities
are contained in the varying intensities of the images on
the cloth.

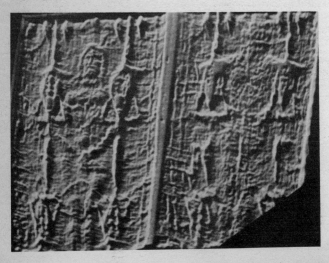

de Poitiers' service as bishop. Evidence, however, does not seem to have been of concern to Canon Chevalier, so intent was he on demolishing even the thought of the Shroud's authenticity.

All of the other documents that Chevalier enlisted to his cause were largely irrelevant or had even less merit than the d'Arcis letter. Those dealing with the foundation of the church at Lirey made no mention of the Shroud at all, and while we may find this perplexing, there are no satisfactory conclusions we can draw from them. Most of the other documents were produced as a result of the d'Arcis letter, and are proof of nothing other than the rough chronology of the Shroud from the time it was made public as a possession of the de Charny family.

Unfortunately, however, those who sought to challenge the didactic conclusions of Canon Chevalier at the time could match him in neither intellect nor wit. His imposing reputation coupled with his brilliant scholastic fire dance on the facts —or lack thereof—had a chilling effect on serious interest in the Shroud. Chevalier received a gold medal for his exposé of the spurious relic, and most reputable scholars wrote the Shroud off as one of the more bizarre curiosities of church history and went on to more serious endeavors.

If Chevalier had not done enough damage, enter now, again in the early 1900s, the Reverend Herbert Thurston, a feisty English Jesuit who liked nothing better than a public, intellectual brawl. Today, Thurston's dissertations on the Shroud—which very closely followed the lines of Chevalier's theses—emerge as little more than severely dated footnotes to the story. But because of his attacks on the authenticity of the Shroud and his critical dismissal of it in the influential *Catholic Encyclopaedia,* Thurston almost single-handedly stifled discourse on the Shroud in the English-speaking world for many years. (Prior to the televised exposition of the Shroud in November 1973, and the subsequent publicity, it was estimated that only one out of twenty people in the Christian world knew anything at all about the Shroud.)

It has been stated that history is the worst enemy of the Shroud. Certainly some historians have been its enemy, if only because their attacks severely curtailed serious academic study for so many years. But do the objections of the historians have any merit at all?

It has been charged that the Shroud has no documented, uninterrupted history from its mention in the Gospels until its surfacing as a possession of the de Charny family in the fourteenth century. It is possible that Dr. Wilson's study of the Edessan Image will substantially reduce the "lost millennium" criticism; but even if it does not, the Shroud does exist, and it is its own most impressive evidence. On it is the image of a crucified man. Analysis of the cloth indicates that it could date to the time of Jesus. Does its lack of pedigree, then, make it any less real? It does not; it merely means that history, in this case, can offer support to neither authenticity nor fabrication.

It has been charged that Pierre d'Arcis' letter to Clement VII fully proves that the Shroud is a fake. As we have seen, the letter does no such thing, and as evidence it is virtually worthless without supporting documentation. But even if documentation did exist—if there were a record of Henri de Poitiers' having conducted an investigation, and of an artist having testified that he painted the Shroud—we would still be left with the plaguing question of how that artist accomplished a feat so complicated and requiring so much knowledge that, to this date, it cannot be duplicated by any process known to man.

Finally, it has been charged that even those involved in the controversy over the Shroud in the fourteenth and fifteenth centuries, including members of the de Charny family, did not believe in its authenticity. Summoned forth as evidence are all the documents which refer to the Shroud as a "representation" of the burial cloth of Christ. This is, of course, the weakest argument of all, for if twentieth-century experts of many and varied disciplines have not yet been able to satisfactorily determine the authenticity or fraudulence of the Shroud, then certainly the unqualified opinions of people living in the Middle Ages, influenced by all the misconceptions and prejudices of that time, have no merit whatsoever.

History, then, cannot now settle the case of the Shroud, and if there are to be satisfactory answers to the centuries-old puzzle, we must turn to science, to the coldly rational examination of the only real document of importance—the Shroud itself.

VIII

The Believer and the Agnostic:
Two Scientists
in Search of the Truth

While Canon Chevalier was basking in the glory of his largely unchallenged scholarship and accepting kudos from all quarters, there were at least two men who had not forgotten the Shroud. Rather, they had taken the study of it from the realms of the church and the historian into the glaring light of the scientific laboratory. Chevalier's earlier pronouncement aside, that light would prove bright indeed.

Like Secondo Pia, whose remarkable photographs had thrust the study of the Shroud into the modern age, Paul Joseph Vignon seemed admirably suited for the task at hand. While published records of Vignon's personal life are scant, John Walsh's account in *The Shroud*, based on interviews with members of Vignon's family, does offer some interesting insights. Born to wealth in Lyon, France, in 1865, Vignon was able to pursue a multiplicity of interests without the burden of financial considerations. He loved to go mountain-climbing, and he vigorously pursued the sport until 1895, when a physical and nervous breakdown brought on by his relentless challenge of the most dangerous peaks forced him to exchange his athletic prowess for more sedate, if no less challenging, pursuits.

As Walsh ironically points out, on some of his mountain forays, "Vignon had for companion another dedicated mountaineer, a young Italian priest named Achille Ratti. Thus, the lure of the mountains had brought together, briefly, the two men who were to become the leading modern advocates of the Shroud of Turin. Years later they met again in a private-audience room at the Vatican—Vignon as the moving spirit in the scientific study of the relic, and Ratti as the learned Pope Pius XI, who believed wholeheartedly in its authenticity."

Vignon's illness was fortuitous, for during his convalescence in Switzerland, he took up painting as therapy, and soon found himself an accomplished artist, displaying his works in a distinguished Paris salon.

About a year after his recovery, Vignon met Yves Delage. Delage was one of France's foremost scientists, an internationally acclaimed zoologist, associate director of the Laboratory for Research in Experimental Zoology, a professor at the Sorbonne, a director of the Museum of Natural History and a member of the powerful and distinguished French Academy of Sciences. Eleven years Vignon's senior, Delage was also a well-known agnostic whose frequent statements on many religious matters were quite acerbic. Vignon was a practicing Catholic.

If their disparate religious leanings were ever an issue between the two men, there is no record of it, and it is likely that they served as perfect

foils to each other during the time they devoted
to the study of the Shroud. Unlike Chevalier, both
men were prepared to drop preconceived notions
the moment they entered the laboratory. What
would emerge from their study would be the
truth, or the closest scientific experimentation
could come to it.

Shortly after their first meeting Vignon's interest in biology was reawakened by Delage, and the
younger man soon joined his mentor on the staff
of *The Biological Year*, a magazine Delage
founded and edited. Later, Vignon became Delage's personal assistant, then took up his own
instructorship in biology at the Sorbonne.

Vignon had seen Pia's photographs of the
Shroud—most literate men of the time had—but
after Chevalier's attacks were made public, Vignon dismissed the whole issue as unworthy of
further pursuit. Not so Delage. As a scientist, he
could not remove the power and reality of the
images from his mind; his family told John Walsh
that he was "disturbed" by them. To the agnostic
Delage, Chevalier's historical "proof" of the
Shroud's forgery must have seemed to be just one
more church-related fallacy of the type Delage so
loved to explode. If the explosion of this one might
placate critics of his agnosticism, at least he would
once again demonstrate that religious questions
would be better answered by unbiased scientific
exploration than by the self-serving and disputable
contentions of exegetes and scholars.

Thus, at Delage's instigation, Vignon and several other scientists set about to investigate the
Shroud. Was it a painting, a forgery, as Chevalier
and others insisted? Or was it something else?
If it were something else, would there be a natural,

physical explanation that could be proven, or at least determined, in a laboratory? Was the figure imprinted on the Shroud the historical personage of Jesus?

The details of Vignon's experiments and findings are to be found in his book *The Shroud of Christ,* published in 1902. (Few copies of the English translation remain; one is in the collection of the New York Public Library.)

Vignon first went to visit Secondo Pia, who explained exactly how he had taken his photographs and gave Vignon several of his best copies. If Vignon wondered whether Pia had in some way faked the negative image, his suspicions were soon dispelled, for Vignon located several other photographs—albeit of poor quality—taken by others and corroborating the negative Shroud image.

As an artist, Vignon realized that the realism of the negative image was equal or superior to the best paintings of the Renaissance. But even if such a picture *could* have been painted in the fourteenth century, why would it have been painted in the negative? The very concept of negativity was unknown until photography was invented, and a fourteenth-century forger would surely have been working to produce something acceptable and believable in his own time, not for the benefit of twentieth-century scientists. In addition, the position of the nail—in the wrist rather than in the palm of the hand—was in conflict with artistic tradition, and the naked figure would surely have shocked the sensibilities of the faithful.

But if the Shroud had not been painted in the

negative, perhaps it was reproduced by traditional application of colors to the linen and the image reversal induced by a chemical transformation of the colors at some later date. Some critics did in fact make this charge, but records of what the image looked like in earlier times are so sparse that no conclusions can be drawn from them. To refute the possibility of chemical transformation, Vignon cited a fresco in the Upper Church of Saint Francis at Assisi. The painting is attributed to Cimabue, and its light values have in fact been reversed by the action of sulfur on the lead base of the paints. But Vignon justly claimed that the image of the Shroud is monochromatic and had not been colored by the application of paint. Thus there could be no question of two colors reversing with the passage of time or, as many had thought, in the heat of the fire at Chambéry in 1532.

Still anxious to dismiss the possibility of the Shroud being a painting, Vignon obtained pieces of linen closely approximating the weave and thickness of the Shroud. He painted them with both oils and watercolors, using the lightest wash that would produce definable images. After the paintings had dried, folding them or rolling them up produced the results one might expect: the paint crumbled and fell off. If the Shroud were the work of an artist, Vignon concluded, then it must have been made with a wash of dye that diffused into the cloth itself, and such dyes would not have been subject to chemical changes that could produce the negative characteristics of the image.

But if the imprints on the Shroud were not the work of an artist, could they have been produced by direct contact with a human body? Vignon donned a false beard, covered himself with fine red chalk, and lay down on a table in his laboratory. His assistants coated a strip of linen with albumen to pick up the chalk impression and draped the cloth over him. The parts of the body that did not touch the sheet left no marks at all; those that did were grossly distorted. The face, over which the sheet had been smoothed down, left no imprint comparable in accuracy and detail to that on the Shroud.

Vignon and his assistants repeated the experiment several times, with variations in method and with great care, but they could not produce a satisfactory image. The image on the Shroud is perfect in its reproduction of anatomical detail. What Vignon got were nothing more than crude, distorted caricatures.

If Vignon and his associates, with all the artistic and scientific knowledge of the twentieth century, could not produce a negative image on cloth, is it conceivable that some fourteenth-century forger produced a work that confounds us even today?

Vignon believed that he had successfully discounted the forgery theory, but he went further to prove the Shroud's authenticity. To do so, he required a scientifically acceptable explanation for the negative image. It was at this point that he began hypothesizing that the imprints were formed by a physico-chemical process that could approximate the qualities of photography. Perhaps, Vignon reasoned, the body could have projected the image, which varied in intensity depending upon the distance of projection, onto the

Shroud which had somehow been sensitized to react much like a photographic plate does.

Working with a friend, René Colson, a professor of physics at the Ecole Polytechnique in Paris, Vignon tried to determine the practicality of his unique idea. His reading of the Gospels led him to believe that the Shroud had been anointed with myrrh and aloes, common aromatics that were frequently used in burial rites. In reading further Colson found an ancient recipe that indicated the myrrh and aloes were pounded with olive oil to form a paste which was then smeared on the burial cloth. An emulsion of aloes in olive oil would yield aloetine, and a cloth soaked in aloetine would brown under the influence of alkaline vapors. Now the two scientists had their sensitized cloth, their "photographic plate." All they had to find would be the origin of the alkaline vapors.

Vignon and Colson knew that vaporized ammonia can project images—they had performed tests to be sure—and when they consulted with chemists, they learned that a body in a crisis of pain emits what is called morbid sweat. They also learned that the body produces a chemical compound called urea, which accumulates in the body fluids as a by-product of protein metabolism. Normal sweat contains some urea, but morbid sweat is highly charged with it. Upon fermentation, urea becomes carbonate of ammonia, and carbonate of ammonia gives off exactly the kind of alkaline vapors that could produce an image like that on the Shroud.

The two scientists went back into the laboratory, and fresh experiments lent substance to their hypothesis. Their best results were obtained by moistening a plaster cast of a hand with ammonia, inserting it into a kid glove and exposing it to a cloth soaked with aloetine. The print thus obtained showed the mass of each finger, but was graduated with such delicacy that no lines of division appeared. Experiments with larger objects, such as plaster heads, were far less successful, mainly because merely moistening plaster with ammonia produced too fast and free a flow of vapors. But it would not have been impossible to duplicate the conditions under which the Shroud's image had been formed, and even the moderate success of Vignon's experiments assured him that he was correct.

He had a burial shroud sensitized by some combination of spices and oils to act as a photographic plate. He had, in the crucifixion of Jesus, a body tortured and wracked with pain. And he had a feasible chemical process that could project an image on the sensitized cloth. Paul Joseph Vignon thought he had eliminated the most perplexing mystery of the Shroud—he knew how its image had been formed. His findings would become known as the vaporograph theory. Vignon would go further in his investigations before making his discovery public, but the vaporographic theory would be his most impressive achievement.

On April 21, 1902, Yves Delage stood before the crowded assembly of the august French Academy of Sciences. As John Walsh writes:

The French Academy was, without doubt, the foremost scientific body in the world at the time, and this room was steeped in long

tradition. Statues and paintings of the greats
of French science and literature peered down
from the wooden paneling, emphasizing a
sense of continuity with the past that was
almost tangible. Only a decade before, one of
these weekly meetings had witnessed the first
presentation of the basic electrical phenomenon that had led to wireless telegraphy.
Interestingly it was before a similar gathering
in 1839, that the technique of photography itself was first given to the world by Daguerre.
There still lingered in the atmosphere dramatic memories of Louis Pasteur, especially
of the famous meeting at which he had announced his vaccine for rabies. That had
been nearly fifteen years before—the last
time the hall had accommodated such a
crush of listeners.

Delage, aware of the singular importance of
the occasion, began reading the paper that he
and Vignon had prepared. After discussing the
history and properties of the Shroud, he detailed
the step-by-step research and experiments of
Vignon and his colleagues, work which Delage
had overseen and approved. Science had shown
the Shroud was not and could not be a painting;
science had demonstrated the Shroud was not a
forgery; science had even determined how the
image was formed.

Delage went on: "Let us add to this, that, in
order for the image to have formed itself without
being ultimately destroyed, it was necessary that
the corpse remain in the Shroud at least twenty-
four hours, the amount of time needed for the

formation of the image, and at the most several days, after which putrefaction sets in, which destroys the image and finally the Shroud." Delage paused, aware of the impact of his next statement, particularly coming from him. "Tradition —more or less apocryphal, I would say—tells us that this is precisely what happened to Christ; dead on Friday and disappeared on Sunday. The man of the Shroud was Christ."

There were more details, to be sure, but Delage's conclusions had been stated, firmly and with absolute conviction. As a man of science and as an agnostic, he believed in the authenticity of the Shroud.

Delage's presentation caused a major sensation in scientific, intellectual and religious circles. The secretary of the Academy refused to print in the *Comptes rendus* (the official proceedings of the Academy) any part of the presentation that asserted the image on the Shroud was that of Jesus. A secret committee of the Academy rejected Delage's request that a more complete investigation of the Shroud be instigated under its auspices. And the international press took up the story with such fervor that the earlier attention accorded Secondo Pia's photographs seemed pale in comparison.

Vignon and Delage were attacked one day and praised the next. Years later, criticism would come from other serious scientists who had done their own research; but at the time, most critics reacted hysterically, grasping at any and every contradictory theory they could summon.

Delage, somewhat taken aback by the savagery of the controversy he had unleashed, expressed himself once more, in a letter to *Revue Scienti-fique*. He said, in part:

> I willingly recognize that none of these given arguments offers the features of an irrefutable demonstration; but it must be recognized that their sum constitutes a bundle of imposing probabilities, some of which are very close to being proven. . . . A religious question has been needlessly injected into a problem which in itself is purely scientific, with the result that feelings have run high, and reason has been led astray. If, instead of Christ, there were a question of some person like a Sargon, an Achilles or one of the pharaohs, no one would have thought of making any objections. . . . I have been faithful to the true spirit of science in treating this question, intent only on the truth, not concerned in the least whether it would affect the interests of any religious party. . . . I recognize Christ as a historical personage and I see no reason why anyone should be scandalized that there still exists material traces of his earthly life.

Several months later, Delage returned to other scientific pursuits. His study of the Shroud was only one aspect of a long and distinguished career. Vignon, however, spent the rest of his life studying the Shroud, making significant contributions to several other areas of Shroud research, most notably the increasingly important iconographic argument. And even if the vaporograph theory seems less and less plausible in light of the more sophisticated knowledge we now have of the

Shroud images, it must be recognized that had it not been for the furor caused by Delage and Vignon, the Shroud would have long since passed into oblivion.

IX

The Second Set of Photographs

For thirty-three years, from June 2, 1898, until May 3, 1931—throughout the height of the public controversy over the Shroud—the venerable cloth had remained hidden, locked in its silver casket above the altar of the Royal Chapel of Turin.

Those who had joined in the controversy during this period had no opportunity to see the Shroud and had worked from copies of Secondo Pia's photograph. Following Yves Delage's presentation of Vignon's findings and the publication of Vignon's book, Canon Chevalier severely rebuked Vignon for invoking the methods of the natural sciences in dealing with an object he had never seen. But of course the indefatigable historian recognized no such compunctions when promoting his own theories.

Father Thurston, while praising the scientific rigor of Vignon's investigation, charged that Pia's black-and-white photograph could be misleading with respect to the issue of the color of the image and the possibility of some sort of color reversal. Thus, until the historical question was settled, Vignon's theory was only of academic value. Since Thurston believed the Shroud was a fourteenth-century forgery, he was merely giving Vignon's work a polite brush-off, though he had at least attempted to deal with Vignon's theory.

Although any number of petitions requested that the Shroud be made available for study during the early part of the twentieth century, all were either rejected or ignored. If certain members of the church hierarchy or of the royal House of Savoy had looked at it, for whatever reasons, there are no records of their impressions. In 1931, however, the king's son, Crown Prince Humbert, was to be married, and the House of Savoy planned to celebrate the joyous national occasion with the public exposition of their most prized possession.

As in 1898, millions of faithful Christians endured long lines to see it. In addition, the king responded—somewhat gingerly—to the many petitions for greater scrutiny. Scientists were still not allowed to study the Shroud firsthand, but the king did grant permission for a new set of photographs to be taken. The availability of a wide variety of modern cameras and sophisticated equipment would ensure technical perfection. The cardinal of Turin, Maurilio Fossati, chose Giuseppe Enrie, who was regarded as one of Italy's best photographers, to take the pictures. Joining Enrie as consultants were Secondo Pia and Paul Vignon, the two men who had until that time done the most to solve the mystery of the Shroud.

Enrie made a number of photographs, the most important of which are a three-section blowup of the entire Shroud, a life-sized reproduction of the face, a smaller shot of the shoulders and back and a seven-to-one enlargement of the area around the wound in the left hand.

All of Enrie's photographs were taken in the

presence of a large number of witnesses; all were developed immediately in a special sacristy darkroom; and all were compared with the Shroud by a panel of experts who pronounced them faithful in every detail to their subject. To guard against a repeat of the charges of fakery that had earlier been leveled at Secondo Pia, a set of affidavits, sworn before a notary, was drawn up, attesting that the photographs were genuine and official.

The new photographs confirmed the legitimacy of Pia's work and portrayed all the aspects of the Shroud with great clarity and detail. The blowup of the wrist area supported Vignon's contention that there was no evidence of paint or other coloring applied to the surface of the cloth. The image, however it had been made, was subtly diffused into the cloth itself. The same photograph afforded textile authorities the basis to classify the cloth as one that could have been common in Jesus' time and one that was not in use in Europe at any time during which the Shroud could have been forged there. In addition, copies of Enrie's photographs were soon dispatched to every corner of the world and became the basis for the great body of scientific study that has continued to the present. (The photographs of the Shroud in this book are copies made from the originals by one of Enrie's successors, and so closely are they protected that anyone using them for reproduction must certify that they will not be retouched or altered in any way.)

Even after Enrie took and developed the photographs, and after the signing of experts' affidavits attesting to the true affinity between the Shroud and the photographs, some scholars still maintain that the photographs are not an adequate basis for legitimate scientific study of the Shroud. And while there are few scientists who would not give their right arm to be able to work from the actual cloth, the arguments of the critics on this point are completely without merit. None of the studies which are accepted as legitimate have exceeded the bounds of the photographic evidence, and all those involved admit that not until a number of sophisticated tests have been conducted on the actual cloth will there be a conclusive determination of its authenticity. But, as Werner Bulst puts it:

Photography is one of the most important tools of investigation used by modern science to approach an object. For photography reproduces any object, in the realm of the visible world, with strict fidelity to nature. In the case of a practically two-dimensional object, like a cloth, the object stands out all the more perfectly in a photograph. Furthermore, photography makes it possible to see much that cannot be detected at all by the human eye, through enlargement, intensification of contrast, use of color filters and properly sensitized film [or plates]. In the case of the Cloth of Turin, it was precisely this that first chanced upon the negative characteristics of the image on the linen fabric. Photography likewise enables anyone at all to examine and test the result wherever he wants. Furthermore, theologians should leave it to scientists to judge the principles and methods of scientific investigation. To date, the latter have expressed no misgivings about using the photographs of Enrie.

Concerning the validity of scientific investigation based on photographs, the author has repeatedly questioned specialists, particularly in the field of forensic medicine and chemistry, the field of the history of textiles and art, and in every instance this procedure has received unequivocal approval.

In fact, forensic medicine, which has something vital to say on the possible authenticity of the Cloth of Turin, makes extensive use of photographs nowadays, and precisely by this very means settles a high percentage of its cases. But rarely does it have at its disposal photographs of the size and quality taken by Enrie. The expert in forensic medicine frequently meets in his work with a situation similar to that found till now in the study of the Cloth of Turin: for extrinsic reasons he is unable to handle the substance of the article to be examined, so that, among other things, chemical analysis is precluded. And yet, despite this, reliable results are often achieved.

As the exposition of 1931 drew to a close, study was beginning on Enrie's photographs that would yield results far more compelling than anything previously known.

X

Dr. Pierre Barbet:
A Surgeon at Calvary

Following the 1931 exposition, a number of men in many different fields of study began intensive examination of the Shroud, working primarily from Enrie's photographs. Not the least of these was Dr. Pierre Barbet, whose medical and anatomical experiments have provided the most comprehensive evidence for the authenticity of the Shroud yet compiled.

Of all those men who have contributed to the story of the Shroud, Barbet is the one about whom fewest personal details are known. What is known of his life serves as little more than a fragmentary footnote to the impressive work he did. His professional qualifications, however, are firmly established and impeccable. Born in 1883, he was surgeon general of the renowned Saint Joseph's Hospital in Paris for thirty-five years and was particularly admired for the proficiency of his surgical skills. In addition, he was a formidable expert on anatomy and had taught that subject for many years.

In 1931 Dr. Barbet was approached by a clergyman friend, Father Armailhac, with a set of Enrie's photographs. The priest sought the opinion of the surgeon and anatomist to provide answers that had eluded theologians and historians. Paul Vignon had tried earlier to answer some of the medical questions, but Pia's photographs—from which Vignon had worked—lacked the clarity and detail of Enrie's. And while Vignon had advanced some opinions, they were not considered to be authoritative.

Barbet's studies lasted some fifteen years, and in the end touched on every aspect of the Shroud. But his most important work—the physiological and anatomical investigations—was conducted between 1932 and 1935. In 1933 Pope Pius XI declared a holy year and petitioned the king of Italy for a new exposition of the Shroud. During that exposition Barbet was allowed to observe the cloth at close range, thus confirming and adding to the knowledge he had already gleaned from the photographs.

During the course of his studies, Barbet published a number of pamphlets and articles. One of these, "The Corporal Passion of Jesus Christ," published in 1940, presented a vivid, graphic re-creation of the Passion, based on Barbet's experiments. By and large, however, his earlier works were written for his sophisticated medical colleagues and were beyond the comprehension of the average layman. Realizing this, in 1950 he published *La Passion de N.-S. Jésus Christ selon le Chirugien*, which covered the whole of his studies and simplified them as much as possible. The English translation, titled *A Doctor at Calvary*, was published in 1953, and is probably the best known of all books on the Shroud. (While indispensable to serious sindonologists, the book is still quite technical, and its translation, I am told by authorities, is not only bad, but also misleading in places. In addition, some of Barbet's historical and archaeological findings are not nearly as authoritative as his medical studies are, and the former should be approached with caution.)

To deal with Barbet's findings as clearly and as simply as possible, it is best to take them one point at a time, not necessarily in the order in which they are presented in his book.

THE DISTINCTION BETWEEN THE BODY IMAGES AND THE BLOODSTAINS

At the exposition of 1933, Dr. Barbet was able to see at first hand the pronounced differences between the appearance of the body images and that of the bloodstains. He had already amassed a solid block of evidence from the photographs, but they were in black and white, and his study of the distinctively different colorations on the cloth reinforced his position. First, he noted the mistlike quality of the body images, so diffused into the cloth that there are no lines of demarcation, contours or shadows, just subtle variations in the light and shade of the brownish stains. In contrast, the bloodstains are much richer in color and have more precise outlines. Barbet also noted that the bloodstains appear thicker at the edges, and that in some places they are "surrounded by an aureole of a much paler color, like a sort of halo." These "halos," he believed, were produced by the serum which separates from the cellular mass of blood as it congeals. Every other detail of the bloodstains on the Shroud matched what Barbet knew to be true in nature. Further, he pointed out that on the Shroud the bloodstains appear as positive images, while the body appears as a negative (see Plate 6). Thus, he concluded, the blood which flowed from the wounds coagulated on the skin and was transferred to the cloth by direct contact, yielding the positive images, as one would expect. The body images, however, had been "projected" in some way, and appear as negative images.

That a fourteenth-century artist could have duplicated the complexities of blood coagulation so perfectly, without making a single mistake, was beyond Barbet's comprehension. And he seriously doubted that even the most skilled medical man could have faked it without detection.

THE PRELIMINARY SUFFERINGS

By studying all of the marks that appear on the Shroud, Barbet was able to isolate and identify the wounds caused prior to the crucifixion. In every case his medical diagnosis corresponded exactly with the record of the Passion as reported in the Gospels or as determined by archaeological investigation.

On the face of the Shroud Dr. Barbet found a number of excoriations, wounds in which the skin is broken. These are particularly noticeable on the right side of the face, and seem to have been caused by blows with a stick approximately 1¾ inches in diameter. The most prominent of these is below the right eye-socket, but there are others on the left cheek and on the lower lip. Barbet also detected a fractured nose.

All over the body, from the shoulders to the lower part of the legs and particularly visible on the dorsal image, are wounds produced by the scourging with the Roman *flagrum*. Barbet noted that all these wounds have a uniform shape and size, and appear as two circles (the balls of lead or bone) joined by a line (the thong that held the balls). He counted as many as one hundred and twenty of these, and he concluded that the wounds resulted from sixty strokes with a double-thonged *flagrum*. He also pointed out that additional strokes might have been administered, but on the Shroud the only ones visible are those which actually broke the flesh. He further reasoned, from the angle of the wounds (which are not the same on both sides of the body), that they were inflicted by two men.

From the ring of bloodstains that encircles the head, Barbet determined that there was, indeed, a crown of thorns. There is no image on the Shroud of the top of the head; blank cloth separates the frontal and dorsal images. But if the crown of thorns were a cap rather than a circlet, why would there not be bloodstains or even a faint image? Barbet believed that the top of the head was covered by a handkerchief joined under the chin, the purpose of which would have been to keep the mouth closed in death against the forces of rigor mortis. Thus the handkerchief absorbed the blood before it could be transferred to the Shroud and also prevented the formation of a body image at this point.

The most evident blood is found on the back of the head. Barbet reasoned that this was perfectly natural, since in the throes of agony Jesus' head would have frequently pitched back against the cross, making large, deep wounds. Again based on his surgeon's knowledge of how blood flows

and coagulates, Barbet concluded that every mark
produced by the crown of thorns is absolutely true
to nature, and could not possibly have been
painted or faked.

Next he turned to three broad patches of
wounds: at the level of the left shoulder blade, at
the knees and across the right shoulder. These,
he believed, were caused directly or indirectly by
Jesus' carrying of the crossbeam up the rugged
terrain to Calvary. The crossbeam would have
been heavy and roughly hewn, and during the
long walk up Calvary, it would have rubbed and
chafed violently across the right shoulder on
which it rested. Every time Jesus fell, the length
of the crossbeam behind him would have struck
his back a glancing, chafing blow, which would be
further inflamed as he struggled to rise under his
burden. Also as Jesus fell, the scattered, jagged
rocks on the road must have scratched and cut
into the flesh of his knees.

Taking this thesis even further, Barbet pointed
to the so-called Holy Coat of Argenteuil. This
cloak, housed in the parish church of Argenteuil,
France, and believed to have been brought there
by Charlemagne, is traditionally accepted as "the
seamless garment of Christ," worn during his ordeal before the crucifixion, and for which the Roman soldiers cast lots after the crucifixion.

In 1934 the coat was photographed, using infrared equipment, by Gérard Cordonnier, a friend
of Barbet and member of the French Regiment of
Engineers. On his photograph, what are believed
to be bloodstains show up in the same places as
Barbet identified them on the Shroud. The accuracy of their placement was further confirmed by
reproducing the stains from the coat on a tunic

of the same dimensions, and placing the tunic on a man about six feet in height, which is believed to be Jesus' height as determined by the images on the Shroud. Again Barbet's theory was upheld. (It should be noted here that I have not been able to find corroborating evidence of this comparative experiment or evidence other than traditional affirmations that the Holy Coat of Argenteuil is authentic. Certainly, however, when the Shroud is finally tested with sophisticated instruments, this coat should be put to those same tests, if only as a supportive measure in the authentication of the Shroud.)

THE WOUNDS IN THE HANDS

According to Gospel descriptions, artistic tradition and popular belief, the wounds in Jesus' hands were caused by the nails driven through the palms. But the evidence of the Shroud, and of physical reality, contradicts these sources, and it is precisely with regard to these wounds that Dr. Barbet made one of his most important discoveries.

On the Shroud, the left hand completely overlaps the right wrist, so that only one wound is visible—through the left wrist. The wound is clear, having formed a round image from which there are several streams of blood. Similar trickles of blood appear on the right forearm.

To prove that crucifixion could not possibly have been successful by nailing the palms to the crossbeam, Barbet took an amputated arm from a cadaver, drove a nail through the palm and suspended a weight of eighty-eight pounds from the elbow. This weight he took to be approximately half that of a man six feet tall. Within minutes, the force of the weight had ripped completely through the palm, and Barbet's device crashed to the floor. And this was dead weight, still and undisturbed. In actuality, the writhing and contortions of the victim would have produced far greater force, exercised in a number of directions. But if the nails were not driven through the palms, then where else and by what means did they accomplish their task?

The wrist is a complex of bones and muscles, and Barbet could not at first figure out how a nail could have been inserted. It would have to be in a place that would secure the body and at the same time be free of bones that would deflect the nail. Comparing the position of the wound on the Shroud to anatomical reality, he found that the wound was centered directly behind the ridge of the upper palm, at the most prominent bending fold of the wrist (see Plates 12 and 13). In exactly that spot is a fleshy space, quite small, which is bounded by four major bones. This gap is called by anatomists the Space of Destot, after the French physician who located and identified it. But the space is small—too small, thought Barbet—to allow the uninterrupted journey of the nail.

Again using the arm of a cadaver, Dr. Barbet carefully marked the spot of the wound and drove a nail through it. He repeated the experiment again and again, and each time he got the same results: the nail passed through easily, finding the natural channel by slightly moving aside the surrounding bones, breaking none, and merely enlarging the space. Thus surrounded by bones and ligaments, the nail would have held firm against even greater pressure than that of a dying man.

Certainly, Barbet mused, experienced executioners would be no strangers to this anatomical intricacy, which must have seemed perfectly suited to their bizarre needs. But could a fourteenth-century forger have such knowledge? Impossible, unless he were a skilled surgeon, centuries ahead of his time.

Dr. Barbet then knew where and how the nails had been driven in, but his experiments also yielded a surprise for which even he, with all his medical experience and sophistication, was not prepared. On the Shroud, although the backs of both hands are clearly visible, neither thumb can be seen (see Plate 11). Many critics of the Shroud's authenticity had pointed to this anomaly in declaring the Shroud a fraud. Such an "error" could not possibly have happened in reality; this had to be the bumbling of the forger, they said.

But every time Barbet had driven a nail into the freshly amputated wrist of a cadaver, he observed that "at the moment when the nail went through the soft anterior parts, the palm being upwards, the thumb would bend sharply and would be exactly facing the palm. . . ." In dissection of the arms, Barbet learned that the trunk of the median nerve was always seriously injured by the penetration of the nail. And this "mechanical stimulation" of the median nerve—which is also the motor, or sensory, nerve—caused the contraction of the thenar muscle, which controls the movement of the thumb.

Could a forger have known that? asked Barbet. And even if he had, would he have dared to portray this obscure physiological quirk that would not be identified and understood for centuries? It does not seem likely.

Not content to stop there, Barbet next studied the blood which had flowed from the wrist wounds. The shape of the bloodstains bothered him, for it seemed that the blood had flowed in several different directions. From a careful study of the angles of the flow, he determined that the body had alternately taken two different positions on the cross (see Plate 10). His explanation of this is both complex and graphic.

When the wrists were nailed to the crossbeams, the arms were outstretched at a ninety-degree angle to the vertical post of the cross. As soon as these nails were in place, the executioners removed their support of the body and, hanging only from the wrist nails, it sagged, causing the arms to drop from their perpendicular angle to one of sixty-five degrees. It was in this position that the blood flowed from the wrist toward the elbow in a more-or-less linear path; and since the blood flow appears primarily in this direction, it would seem that this was the predominant position of the body on the cross. However, some trickles of blood also flowed at angles of between sixty-eight and seventy degrees, indicating that the body had raised itself slightly from time to time, thus moving the arms back toward their original horizontal position.

Dr. Barbet postulated these angles by charting the bloodstains on the Shroud, later working them out on geometric graphs and confirming them by experimenting on a cadaver. He knew what had happened, and when he discovered why, he was able to form a theory of exactly how Jesus died.

THE CAUSES OF DEATH

As has already been noted, when Jesus' wrists were nailed to the cross and the support given by the executioners then removed, his body sagged, and his entire weight hung from the wrists. His arms were thus stretched obliquely (at sixty-five degree angles) above his head. Dr. Barbet computed the weight that pulled on each wrist to be two hundred-forty pounds of pressure. Then the feet were nailed, with the legs bent in a slightly flexed position.

In this position, which was the most common in crucifixion, the sides would be relatively immobile; exhalation would be greatly hindered, and the victim would have the sensation of progressive suffocation. The heart would have to work harder, its beats becoming faster and weaker.

Cramps would begin in the forearms, then in the arms, and would finally spread to the lower limbs and the trunk. The lungs would be filled with air but unable to expel it. Thus the normal oxygenation of the circulating blood would not take place, and asphyxiation would begin. The victim would be affected as surely and as drastically as if he were being violently strangled. This same condition, Dr. Barbet explained, is produced by tetanus, through the intoxication of the nerve centers. The combination of symptoms of general contraction is thus called "tetany." Asphyxiation and tetany would cause rapid death.

If such was the case, how then, asked Dr.

Barbet, could victims of crucifixion "escape for the moment from these cramps and this asphyxia, so that they survived for several hours, even for two or three days? This could only be done by relieving the dragging on the hands, which seems to be the initial and determining cause of the whole phenomenon."

There was a way.

Using his feet as a fulcrum, the victim could lift his body and bring his arms back toward their original horizontal position. With the weight of the body thus supported by the muscles in the legs and the nails through the feet, "the dragging on the hands would then be greatly reduced; the cramps would be lessened and the asphyxia would disappear for the moment, through the renewal of the respiratory movements. Then the fatigue of the lower legs would supervene, which would force the crucified to drop again, and bring on a fresh attack of asphyxia. The whole agony was thus spent in an alternation of sagging and then of straightening the body, of asphyxia and respiration."

Once the victim had become so exhausted that he could no longer force himself up on the nails, the prolonged asphyxia in the sagging position would quickly bring on death. According to Dr. Barbet, this is what happened to Jesus, who was already severely weakened by the grueling tortures administered before crucifixion.

Barbet's theory had first been tentatively ventured by his predecessor at Saint Joseph's Hospital, Dr. Le Bec, and had later been amplified by Dr. R. W. Hynek, who had witnessed the same type of death—caused by hanging condemned men from a post by their hands, with their feet scarcely touching the ground—inflicted by the Austro-German Army. The punishment was called *aufbinden,* and was also used by the Nazis at Dachau.

Barbet found that death by asphyxia was:

borne out by the marks which it has left on the Shroud. We might even say that tetany and asphyxia, of which for a doctor there can be no doubt, prove that the imprints on the Shroud conform with reality; this body died the death of a crucified body.

We can indeed see that the great pectoral muscles, which are the most powerful inspiratory muscles, have been forcibly contracted—they are enlarged, and drawn up toward the collarbone and the arms. The whole thoracic frame is also drawn up, and greatly distended, with a *maximum* inspiration. The epigastric hollow (the pit of the stomach) is sunk and pressed inward, through this elevation and this forward and outward distension of the thorax. . . . The diaphragm, which is a great inspiratory muscle, would also tend to raise the epigastrum in a normal abdominal respiration. With this distension and this forced elevation of the sides, it can only move back toward the abdominal mass; and that is why, above the crossed hands, the hypogastrium, the lower abdomen, can be seen protruding.

Barbet also used this theory to explain the two directions of the blood flow on the forearms. The major long, slender flow that runs from the wrist almost to the elbows would have occurred when the body was in the sagging position. The smaller trickles, which can be described as moving toward the ground when the arms were in the almost horizontal position, would have occurred during the times Jesus raised himself to relieve the asphyxia.

Barbet's theory is further supported by the normal method of insuring the rapid death of crucified victims—the breaking of the legs. This practice has been verified by historical and archaeological sources, and it would have prevented the victim from raising himself to ward off the asphyxia. The only plausible reason that such a procedure was not used in the case of Jesus was that he died so rapidly, it was unnecessary. In his case, therefore, the spear thrust in the side was deemed sufficient to legally verify death so that the body could be delivered to Joseph of Arimathaea.

THE WOUND IN THE HEART

According to the Gospel of John, when the soldiers had determined that Jesus was already dead, "one of the soldiers stabbed his side with a lance, and at once there was a flow of blood and water." On the Shroud, on the left side of the rib cage (on the right side of the body because of image reversal), below the armpit is a heavy stain caused by a gaping wound (see Plate 14). This stain, according to medical authorities, is from a combination of blood and clear, organic fluid.

In earlier times it was commonly believed impossible for blood to flow from a corpse and many churchmen had proclaimed the flow of blood and "water" to be a miracle. As a surgeon who had experimented on and dissected numerous cadavers, Barbet knew that blood does not coagulate in a corpse, but remains liquid until putrefaction sets in. To him, the flow indicated on the Shroud was perfectly natural, considering what he had determined about the wound.

In explaining his findings to laymen, Barbet felt obligated to confront the popular myth that the heart is on the left side. Not so, he said, "the heart is mesial and in front, resting on the diaphragm, between the two lungs. . . . Only its point is definitely to the left, but its base extends to the right beyond the breastbone."

Using the markings of the wound and the bloodstains on the Shroud as his guide, and transferring a duplication of them to the body of a man six feet tall, Barbet hypothesized that the blade of the spear had entered the body above the sixth rib, and had penetrated the pleura (a delicate serous membrane enveloping the lung) and the right lung. Continuing its thrust, the blade then punctured the pericardium (the membranous sac enclosing the heart), and finally pierced the right auricle of the heart (see Plate 15).

In performing experiments on cadavers, Barbet found that blood indeed flowed from the right auricle of the heart, and that the mysterious water could be pericardial fluid, or serum, which had accumulated there. It was released along with blood at the time the wound was inflicted.

Once again medical science attested to the authenticity of the Shroud, and in this case, it also upheld John's sighting of blood and "water."

During his studies, Barbet found something else:

> On the dorsal image of the Shroud, one can see a largish trail at the base of the thorax, stretching the whole way across; on the right side it is fairly broad, and then divides up into little streamlets as it nears the left side of the trunk [See Plate 17]. This trail is caused by a flow of blood. . . . Whence came this blood and why did it flow transversally? Once again, anatomy will give us the reason for this.
>
> At the moment of the blow with the lance the dead body was attached to the cross in a vertical position. The right auricle was able to empty itself and probably also the superior vena cava [a large vein in the heart]. . . . But the inferior vena cava [the other large vein in the heart], which lies below it, has remained full. It is long and broad, and we know that when it is cut in an autopsy there is at once a regular flow of blood in the abdomen.
>
> When Joseph of Arimathaea had taken the body down from the cross, he and whoever helped him would have carried the body, *"horizontally,* to the tomb. The blood of the inferior vena cava would then have flowed back into the right auricle and, going through the tunnel made by the lance, which remained gaping open, would have flowed out. But as the body was horizontal, this fresh flow would slip around the right side and would continue to flow transversally *on the back, going right across the lower part of the thorax."*

Could this phenomenon have been known by a fourteenth-century forger?

The Wounds in the Feet

The wounds in the feet are difficult to study for several reasons. On the frontal image, the knees can be seen clearly, but below them the image becomes gradually less distinct, and the feet virtually invisible. On the dorsal image, the images of the feet are obscured by bloodstains which spread out over the length of both feet (see Plate 20). Nonetheless, from the dorsal image it can be determined that the feet were slightly crossed, with the left in front.

From his studies, computations and practical experiments on cadavers, Barbet believed that on the cross the feet were completely crossed, with the left overlapping the right, and with one nail penetrating both and buried into the hard wood of the cross. His experiments showed that if a nail were driven into the feet of a cadaver at the position the wounds appear on the Shroud, the nail would go through a fleshy spot below what is known as Lisfranc's Spaceline, which separates the tarsus from the metatarsals, between the second and third toes (see Plate 21). If the nail were positioned further toward the tarsus, it would have encountered a mass of bone. If it were any lower, it probably would not have secured the feet to the cross. The images on the Shroud again corresponded with anatomical reality.

In his conclusion to *A Doctor at Calvary*, Dr. Barbet wrote:

I started out with a certain skepticism . . . to examine the images on the Shroud; I was quite ready to deny their authenticity, if they disagreed with anatomical truth.

But, on the contrary, the facts gradually grouped themselves into a bundle of proofs, which carried increasing conviction. Not only was the explanation of the images so natural and simple that it proclaimed them to be genuine; but, when at first they seemed to be abnormal, experiment demonstrated that they were as they should be, that they could not be different, and as a forger would have portrayed them. . . . Anatomy thus bore witness to their authenticity, in full agreement with the Gospel texts.

The surgeon had performed an autopsy on the Passion and on the Shroud. He pronounced them authentic.

Since his experiments and reports, some medical authorities have taken issue with several of Dr. Barbet's conclusions, most notably the cause of death and the "blood and water" that issued from the wound in the side. Although the arguments do not abate, the comments of Dr. Robert Bucklin seem to represent the latest, most authoritative conclusions of the contemporary pathologist:

The source of the blood cannot be seriously questioned, since it must have come from the heart. And from the position of the blood imprint, as well as its structure, it can be assumed that this blood came from the right side of the heart. This chamber was dilated after death, and when pierced by the lance, the blood readily flowed from it. A considerable portion of the blood must have dripped onto the ground, but enough was left to form a large stain on the chest and to be later transferred to the Shroud. The source of the water described by John presents more controversy. One possibility [propounded by Barbet] is that the fluid represented pericardial fluid. However, the amount of pericardial fluid normally present is in the nature of twenty to thirty cubic centimeters, too small an amount to be seen by the naked eye as it came out of the wound in the side with the blood from the heart.

Another theory [held by other medical authorities] is that there was a hydrohemothorax [internal hemorrhage] caused by the trauma to the chest by the scourging and increased by the position of the body on the cross prior to death. By gravity the heavier blood could have separated, leaving two layers, and when the lance pierced the side it released first the blood and then the clear fluid. A combination of the two theories might well explain the situation. An accumulation of fluid in the pleural space without hemorrhage is a logical conclusion as the result of congestive heart failure related to the position of the victim on the cross. It is quite possible that there was a considerable amount of fluid so accumulated, enough that when the lance pierced the side that fluid would be clearly seen. Then by an actual puncture of the heart, there would be an outflow of blood. If the theory of pleural effusion plus puncture of the right side of the heart were sustained, it would be expected that the water would have been visible from the side before the blood and that John's words would have appeared as "water and blood" rather than "blood and water." As a matter of interest, the words appear in the former sequence in several of the early Greek translations of the New Testament.

The final verdict on these medical issues is not yet in. Neither Barbet nor Bucklin nor any other forensic pathologist has had adequate access to the Shroud to render definitive judgments. No chemical analyses for traces of body fluids have yet been conducted. Thus, the important question, for now, is whether the visible wounds on the Shroud result from a human being undergoing the tortures ascribed to the crucifixion of Jesus. All medical figures who have made serious studies believe they are. Could an artist—or even a doctor—have faked those wounds with such fidelity to medical detail? The medical men agree that the wounds could not have been faked.

XI

The Evidence of Jehohanan

When Dr. Barbet conducted his medical studies of the Shroud in the early 1930s, the only knowledge the world had of crucifixion around the time of Jesus came from written records of no great detail, consistency or reliability, and from artistic representations that could by no means be declared historically accurate. Although thousands of men had been crucified during the ancient Roman era, no remains of a crucified victim had ever been found. Such would be the case until 1968.

In June of that year, Israeli builders began excavating for an apartment complex at Giv'at ha-Mivtar, about a mile north of the Damascus Gate of the Old City of Jerusalem. They uncovered three burial caves that housed fifteen limestone ossuaries, all containing human skeletal remains. Of the thirty-five individuals catalogued by anthropologists, five were said to have died by violence. Only one of these five concerns us here.

In the ossuary designated I/4 were found the bones of an adult male in his mid-twenties and of a child. Outside the tomb were two inscriptions bearing the name, presumably, of the adult male —Jehohanan. Jehohanan met his death by crucifixion.

Of the date of execution, Dr. V. Tzaferis of the Israeli Department of Antiquities and Museums says:

Mass crucifixions in Judea are mentioned under Alexander Janneus, during the revolt against the census of A.D. 7, and again during the Jewish revolt which brought about the final destruction of the Second Temple in A.D. 70. Individuals were also crucified occasionally by the Roman procurators. Since the pottery and ossuaries found in Tomb I exclude the period of Alexander Janneus for this crucifixion, and since the general situation during the revolt of A.D. 70 excludes the possibility of burial in Tomb I, it would seem that [Jehohanan] was either a rebel put to death at the time of the census revolt in A.D. 7 or the victim of some occasional crucifixion. It is possible, therefore, to place this crucifixion between the start of the first century A.D. and somewhere just before the outbreak of the first Jewish revolt.

Although Jehohanan's remains were in an extremely poor state of preservation, the information they have yielded has been of great significance, in respect to both our knowledge of crucifixions generally and to the continuing effort at authenticating the Shroud. If Dr. Tzaferis' calculations are correct, and if the crucifixion of Jehohanan was a typical execution—and there is no indication it was not—then at least a reasonable comparison can be made between the crucifixion of Jehohanan and that of Jesus, as evidenced by the markings on the Shroud.

One of the men instrumental in the recovery, reconstruction and study of Jehohanan's remains was Dr. Nicu Haas of the Department of Anatomy, Hebrew University-Hadassah Medical School. Having separated the bones of Jehohanan from those of the child, and having satisfied themselves that there was no evidence of a third individual, Dr. Haas and his colleagues found three specific marks of violence on Jehohanan, all relating directly or indirectly to death by crucifixion. There were no other marks of violence or deformations, and it is believed that Jehohanan had been remarkably healthy.

The most important discovery was two calcaneal (heel) bones pierced and joined by a single, large iron nail. Below the head of the nail, between it and the bones, were the remains of a wooden plaque, hewn from *Pistacia* or *Acacia* wood. The purpose of the plaque would have been to further secure the feet to the cross, prohibiting the faint possibility that the victim might be able to tear his feet from the head of the nail. Because of the positioning of the wooden plaque, with the feet between it and the cross, it could not have been the footrest, or *suppedaneum*, that was used in some crucifixions. The tip of the nail was bent, and on it were found several small granular-nodular fragments which have been identified as olive wood.

If the crucifixion of Jehohanan had been completed without incident or problem, it is highly unlikely that this unusual artifact—the two heel bones still joined by the nail which anchored them to the cross—would exist. But from all the evidence—the bent nail with its fragments of olive wood and the fact that Jehohanan's feet were amputated after his death—it is believed that the nail struck a knot in the olive wood, thus bending it and making it difficult to remove when it came time to take Jehohanan down from the cross. Rather than attempting to remove the whole body, which under the circumstances would have proved incredibly awkward, the executioners simply amputated the feet and carved out the tough chunk of wood, both still attached to the nail. All were then dumped into the tomb with the rest of Jehohanan's remains.

Although the bones of Jehohanan's left arm were too poorly preserved for successful study, on the right radius (a major bone of the forearm) Dr. Haas found evidence of a small scratch that he describes as resembling an incisure produced on fresh bone by compression and friction. He concludes that the scratch was caused by the penetration of a nail between the radius and the ulna (the other major bone of the forearm). Other details of the scratch indicate that the victim must have writhed in anguish toward the end of his ordeal, causing the nail to scrape against the bone.

From severe fractures of the lower leg bones (the tibiae and left fibula), Dr. Haas and his colleagues were able to conclude that Jehohanan received a direct, deliberate blow to the shin area. This blow undoubtedly was issued as the *coup de grâce* or *crurifragium* that insured the rapid death of crucified victims.

After a painstaking and complicated study of all aspects of Jehohanan's remains, Dr. Haas was able to describe the position of the body on the cross: "The feet were joined almost parallel, both transfixed by the same nail at the heels, with the legs adjacent; the knees were doubled, the right one overlapping the left; the trunk was contorted; the upper limbs were stretched out, each stabbed by a nail in the forearm."

As it applies to the Shroud and to the crucifixion of Jesus, the evidence of Jehohanan is circumstantial at best. It must be noted that the crucifixions of Jehohanan and Jesus as analyzed by Drs. Haas and Barbet were marked by some variations. Nonetheless, Jehohanan does provide the only extant conclusive proof of crucifixion methods, and the similarities between his findings and those of Dr. Barbet's findings are obvious.

In both cases, the nails supporting the bodies were not driven through the palms, as has been popularly believed, but through the wrists or forearms, between bones which would have adequately supported the weight of contorted and writhing bodies.

In both cases, one nail secured both feet to the cross, and while these two cases do not conclusively prove that one nail was commonly used, they do provide substantial evidence.

In addition, the *crurifragium* administered to Jehohanan was almost certainly a common practice, and not only lends weight to the Gospel and historical testaments, but also makes the reason that Jesus was spared such abuse—he was already dead—much more compelling.

XII

Can the Shroud Perform Miracles?

The subject of miracles is a highly controversial
one about which most people have opinions,
though none have conclusive answers. There are
certainly those who accept religious miracles just
as they accept the concept of a supernatural God.
Providing much substance, if no proof, to claims
of religious miracles are the numerous nonmed-
ical cures of physical ailments catalogued at the
Roman Catholic shrine of Lourdes in France.

However, there seems to be a popular miscon-
ception that relics or shrines *cause* miracles. According to the doctrine of the Roman Catholic
Church, miracles are caused by supernatural intervention to relieve the suffering of the faithful.
God's all-powerful benevolence and the faith of
the recipient of a miracle are the essential elements, and relics and shrines are only material
symbols through which believers express their
faith and offer their prayers.

Medical doctors have studied "faith healings,"
whether through relics, shrines or the activities of
the so-called healers. The latter are becoming
more and more prominent and are attracting increasing scientific interest. Some cases, of course,
are hoaxes; others reflect radical, if only temporary, remission; while still others indicate genu-

158

ine cures. Some contemporary psychologists translate the "faith" of the recipients of cures into a kind of psychosomatic effect—that is, the emotional condition of the person is, in fact, responsible for the physical change, and while the person may well believe that his cure is the result of supernatural intervention, he has, in effect, cured himself, the psychologists say.

But what of the documented and controlled experiments in which such healers have had a positive or curative effect on plants, enzymes and rats? Can nonhuman subjects also be affected by internal psychosomatics, or are the changes in them produced by some as yet undefinable energy flow from the healers? Although both skeptics and believers may scoff at such reserve, it seems premature either to reject miracles or to accept them. We simply know too little about ourselves and about the forces that affect us to reach hard-and-fast conclusions.

We do know that throughout the documented history of the Shroud, there are a few vague references to miracles attributed to it, but there is so little substance to these stories that meaningful conclusions about them are impossible. In 1692, for instance, it was believed that Turin was spared from the Black Plague as a direct result of appeals to the Shroud. A bronze plaque on a Turin city wall commemorates this "miracle." Obviously, Turin's residents could have been spared from the plague for any number of natural, logical reasons, and a direct correlation involving miracles cannot be ventured at this time.

It seems odd that such an unusual relic, venerated by millions of pilgrims during its limited expositions, is not the subject of countless stories of great wonders. But it is not, and one can only speculate that because it was inaccessible, even during the expositions, rumors were dampened. The reserve with which the church has treated it must have further stunted the growth of miracle stories.

The only documented modern account of a miraculous cure being sought directly through the Shroud occurred in 1955. During the Second World War, British Royal Air Force Captain G. L. Cheshire had been a much-decorated hero. After the war, the publication of his best-selling memoirs, *Bomber Pilot*, made him a national celebrity. A convert to Catholicism, he devoted his life to philanthropic work. Because of his fame and well-publicized philanthropy, on May 11, 1955, he received the following letter, which he later published in his book, *Pilgrimage to the Shroud:*

Gloucester, May 10

Dear Mr. Cheshire:

I am writing to ask you if my daughter Josephine could be blessed with the relic of the Holy Shroud. Josephine is ten years old and she is very ill in hospital—with osteomyelitis in the hip and leg. Also a lung abscess. Her doctor has told me that there is no hope of Josephine getting better. She has been in and out of hospital for the last five years. On Friday she received the last rites of Holy Church. Josephine has asked me to write to you and she said if only she could see the relic she will get better and walk again. Everyone at the hospital has been very good to her. She is always in great pain but she has always got a smile . . .

I know I am asking for great things, but I do hope and pray that my prayers will be answered for my daughter to get better.

I remain,

Mrs. Veronica Woollam

Cheshire was away when the letter arrived, so an assistant in his office answered Mrs. Woollam, saying that the Shroud was in Turin, and that it was not shown to the public except during rare expositions. The assistant also enclosed a photograph of the face on the Shroud.

Upon his return home, Cheshire was sympathetic to the young girl's plea, but believed he could do nothing. Five days later, however, he received another letter from Josephine's mother, this one telling him that the girl was no longer on her death bed, but up and around the hospital ward in a wheelchair. As Cheshire put it, "Someone talked hopefully of a miracle, but this we stopped, pointing out that we had nothing concrete to go on and that in any case for a cure to be recognized as miraculous it must, among other requirements, be complete and permanent. Josie's cure could not be complete, for she was still in hospital."

Two weeks later, "a third letter arrived. Josie had been discharged and was back at home. Moreover, for the first time there was a note of joy—almost of triumph."

On June 17, Cheshire visited the Woollam home without warning. Josie was in her wheelchair and showed him her legs. They were deformed and mutilated, but before the arrival of the photograph of the Shroud they had also been open and running. The receipt of the photograph had coincided with the remarkable remission of the disease.

Although skeptical that actually seeing or touching the Shroud could help the girl fully recover and walk again, Cheshire was astounded at her recovery at that point, and resolved to do everything he could to help.

In July, Cheshire and Josie journeyed to Turin, stopping on the way to get permission from Humbert II for Josie to see and hold the Shroud. While countless other requests had gone unheeded over the years, every effort was made to accommodate Josie. When they arrived in Turin, the ex-king had already telephoned ahead, authorizing the authorities of the archdiocese to grant any reasonable request Josie might make.

A special mass was said on her behalf, and she was allowed to see and hold the Shroud on her lap. There was no miracle; there was no cure. There was, however, a radiant young crippled girl who understood that while she would remain afflicted, she had also done something that few people would ever do—she had touched the Holy Shroud.

It is sad that Josie was not blessed with a miracle or with a cure. But those who may be disappointed about the lack of evidence of Shroud miracles should be cognizant of the attitude of some of the Shroud's most dedicated proponents.

Is it not enough, they ask, that the Shroud exists at all? For if it is authentic, then it is in and of itself the most miraculous of all miracles—a self-portrait of Jesus Christ.

XIII

The Keepers of the Shroud

It is virtually imposible for the intelligent, inquisitive person, no matter what his religious beliefs, to understand the attitude of the Shroud's keepers until recent years. As has already been stated, the Shroud is the private property of Humbert II, the head of the House of Savoy and exiled king of Italy. It is under the care and protection of the Archdiocese of Turin. Theoretically, Umberto can do anything he wishes with the Shroud—leave it where it is, sell it, even destroy it. He is, of course, consulted on any matter that might affect it, but in reality the Archbishop of Turin has almost absolute control over it.

Until 1969, despite constant pleading from responsible men of science and of the church for more study, for scientific testing of the cloth, for greater public access to it and for signs of interest from the clergy who control access to it, the Shroud remained hidden away. Locked in its silver casket, sealed and constantly guarded, it remained in Turin, where it had been since 1578. It had been unseen and untouched by anyone since the exposition of 1933, with the single known exception of the young crippled girl, Josie.

The faithful worshipped in the cathedral; pilgrims visited the Shroud museum in the Archdiocese complex; books and articles were written about the Shroud. But inquiries about it or petitions for further study were either ignored or given evasive, ambiguous replies.

Over the years, many questions have been asked about this intransigent attitude. Is the church afraid that the Shroud is a fake? Are the authorities fearful that it might be destroyed or damaged?

If the Shroud is authentic, then it is the greatest relic known to Christianity. Why, then, are Christians not allowed to see it?

The answers are not forthcoming. John Walsh says:

> For some, this attitude is incomprehensible at best, and at worst it points to a fear of what might be disclosed. The truth is, however, that this problem of physical testing is not a simple one. The Shroud is, after all, a spiritual object, hallowed by the prayers and devotions of many millions of pilgrims, and by the veneration of popes and saints. Its true value is religious, and, if authentic, it goes far beyond even such archaeological wonders as the Rosetta Stone or the clay tablets of Nineveh. Those who have inherited the task of safeguarding it and preserving it into the future feel their obligation heavily. They are

understandably slow to endanger even the
smallest fragment of it.

The Reverend Peter M. Rinaldi is not nearly
so charitable, but then he has spent the greatest
part of his adult life in frustrating efforts to obtain complete authentication of the Shroud and
to publicize it as much as possible. Rinaldi first saw
the Shroud when he was an altar boy in the cathedral of Turin during the exposition of 1933. Until
September 1977, when he returned to Turin to
devote all his time to the cause of the Shroud, he
was pastor of the Corpus Christi Church in Port
Chester, New York. Adjacent to the church, he has
erected a magnificent shrine to "the Christ of
the Holy Shroud," which features a life-sized illu-
minated reproduction of the Shroud. Rinaldi is
also one of the moving forces in the Holy Shroud
Guild, an international group of scholars, scientists
and clergymen whose efforts are devoted to further study and authentication of the Shroud.

Commenting in 1972 on Walsh's explanation
for the attitude of the Turin officials, Rinaldi
said: "These remarks are both well-reasoned and
kind, but they hardly justify the 'iron curtain of
silence' some responsible authorities have clamped
down on the Shroud. Among these authorities, the
jealous or timid custodians of the Shroud's cita-
del in Turin are unquestionably the ones who, for
reasons best known to themselves, have consis-
tently delayed the progress of the Shroud's cause."

Rinaldi is an erudite, gentle man. He is as
knowledgeable about the political ramifications of
the Shroud as he is about the ancient cloth itself.
Despite his outspoken criticism, he has maintained

close personal ties with the officials in Turin. In my numerous conversations with him, I have never heard him raise his voice in anger against their intransigence. His voice is raised in frustration, for Rinaldi cannot understand the many years of silence and inactivity.

It is true that Michele Cardinal Pellegrino, Archbishop of Turin until mid-1977, had been in bad health for several years. It is true that the Turin archdiocese has problems other than those concerning the Shroud. It is true that the Shroud is the object of considerable political pressure from many viewpoints. But these problems cannot conceivably warrant what Rinaldi has called, only partly in jest, "the scandal of the Shroud."

Much of the progress that has been made in recent years is the result of the persistent efforts of Father Rinaldi and Father Otterbein, whose pressure has been unrelenting.

In June of 1969, something finally happened. A small, then secret, panel of experts in many fields—archaeology, chemistry, physics and medicine—was allowed to spend several days examining the Shroud. Although he had been archbishop of Turin for a number of years, Cardinal Pellegrino then saw the Shroud for the first time, and that fact alone indicates his prior lack of interest in the cloth. It might never have been made public that the secret study had taken place at all had it not been for a leak to a strange man who calls himself Kurt Berna, or John Reban. His real name is Hans Naber, and his involvement with the Shroud provides one of the most bizarre episodes in its history. Surprisingly, the usual garden-variety of eccentrics and charlatans who have a special talent for attaching themselves to the unusual and mysterious have stayed away from the Shroud—with the single exception of Hans Naber.

Some years ago, Naber latched onto the issue of the Shroud. The basis for his interest seems to have stemmed from some kind of vision that he claims demonstrated to him that Jesus did not die on the cross. He further claims that the markings on the Shroud prove this. In 1967, Naber—writing under the name John Reban—published a book entitled *Inquest on Jesus Christ* in which he expounded his theories, and which sold briskly in England and in Continental Europe. In the book, his own "studies" were buttressed with the testimony of numerous "scientific experts" who, according to Naber, wished to remain anonymous in order to protect their objectivity.

In fact, the experts remained anonymous because they were nonexistent. Virtually every word that Naber has uttered or written on the subject of the Shroud has been discredited by the investigations of Professor Werner Bulst and Dr. David Willis, a British physician, and it is unfortunate that so many unsuspecting readers, apparently including Naber's English publisher, were taken in.

In 1970 Naber made one last round of headlines with his ridiculous charges. Learning of the secret examination conducted in 1969, Naber used the world press to denounce the study as an attempt on the part of the Roman Catholic Church to destroy the Shroud, his "evidence" that Jesus did not die on the cross.

As absurd as Naber's claims were, they did force the Turin authorities into an awkward and embarrassing position. Yet instead of being immediately forthcoming and candid, Cardinal Pellegrino issued only the briefest of statements about the secret study. It was conducted, he said at the time, merely to determine the condition of the Shroud and to ascertain whether any measures were necessary to protect the cloth against deterioration or damage from Turin's industrial smog. The names of the experts involved were not released at the time "in order to shield them from the kind of publicity that would rather hinder than favor their research."

Although no responsible critic placed the activities of the Turin authorities on the same level as Naber's, their secrecy ironically did fall to some degree into the same pattern. The reports were so guarded that months after the study had been conducted, Umberto complained to Father Rinaldi that he had only seen one of them, and that one only because the expert in question was a personal friend of his.

In fact, the reports, finally released in January 1976 were essentially what the cardinal had proclaimed them to be—analyses of the condition of the cloth and proposals for future study and preservation. More photographs were taken, although their quality, in terms of usefulness to further scientific study, is disappointing. No sophisticated tests were undertaken, and no damage was done. All the members of the investigating group were European scientists, scholars or ranking churchmen of the Archdiocese of Turin.

Following his own observation of the Shroud during the 1969 study, Cardinal Pellegrino's atti-

tude changed, if not for the best, then at least for
the better. Preparations began for some kind of
public exposition of the cloth, and the cardinal
became more receptive to proposals for physical
tests.

On Friday evening, November 23, 1973, the
Shroud was the subject of a televised exposition
that was broadcast in most of Europe and in parts
of South America. The date had been set and
postponed several times, and details that changed
frequently and abruptly were hammered out at
long and agonizing conferences. Months before
the exposition was to take place, I requested permission to be present, along with other members
of the press, concerned scholars, clergy and scientists. I volunteered to obey any strictures that
might be placed on me. I wanted—indeed, I
needed—to see the mysterious ancient cloth that
had for so long occupied my time and my thoughts.
In spite of the efforts of Father Rinaldi on my
behalf, I was told that I would not be allowed
access to the Shroud, that there would be no
press conference and that no one other than the
television crew and Turin officials would be ad-
mitted to the cathedral when the cloth was displayed. I decided not to make the trip to Italy.

As it turned out, however, a press conference
was held prior to the exposition, and a number
of people were allowed to see the Shroud at close
range and to photograph it. Although I was disappointed and my work on this book was hindered,
my experience was nothing more than another
example of the haphazard way affairs relating to
the Shroud have been handled.

During the press conference Cardinal Pellegrino explained why the exposition was to be televised rather than held in public:

The medium of television is a modern and up-to-date technique which makes it possible for millions of people to contemplate the precious relic at the same time. So high a number of spectators could not have been attained at a traditional exposition, which would have involved, among other things, many problems of organization and logistics, and which would have subjected the Shroud to the risk of wear and to the action of substances in the atmosphere. Many people, moreover, would not have been able to come to Turin. Those, especially, who need the comfort of this document of the Passion of Jesus—the poor, the aged, the infirm—would not have had an opportunity to see it.

Cardinal Pellegrino also stressed the religious aspects of the presentation:

The significance and value of the relic are so great as to overcome every legitimate doubt. It must be distinguished from the disputed question of the authenticity of the Holy Shroud. It is a reminder, a most effective reminder, of Him whom all humanity, believing and unbelieving, regards with veneration. It has something to say to everyone.

The exposition, estimated to have reached as many as 200 million people, consisted of six

parts: an introduction by the writer Fortunato
Pasqualino; a videotape of the message of Pope
Paul VI; a videotape of the Shroud being removed from the reliquary; an illustrated history
of the Shroud; general and detailed views of the
Shroud, including positive and negative images
of the face; and an address by Cardinal Pellegrino.

Following is an excerpt from Pope Paul's remarks:

To our venerable brother Michele Cardinal
Pellegrino, Archbishop of Turin, and to all of
the holy and beloved Church entrusted to his
pastoral ministry and in full communion with
us. And to all who are, by means of radio
and television, following this ceremony.

We, too, as though we were present, fix
the gaze of our spirit, in most attentive and
devoted admiration, on the sacred Shroud, of
which a pious and extraordinary exposition
has been arranged at Turin, the custodian of
this singular treasure.

We know how much research is concen-
trated on the celebrated relic, and we are not
unaware of how much fervent and heartfelt
piety surrounds it. We personally still remember the vivid impression that was stamped
upon our spirit when, in May 1931, we had
the good fortune to be present, on the occasion of special observances then being rendered to the Shroud, at a projection of it
upon a large lighted screen; and the face of
Christ, there represented, seemed to us more
true, more profound, more human and divine, than any other image we had been able

to admire and to venerate. This was, for us,
a moment of extraordinary enchantment.

Whatever scientific and historical judgment competent scholars may pass on this
astonishing and mysterious relic, we cannot
refrain from praying that it may not only
bring those who examine it to an intense
physical examination of the exterior and
mortal lineaments of the Savior, but bring
them also to a more penetrating vision of His
fascinating mystery. . . .

What good fortune, then, and what a mystery to see Jesus! Him, Jesus Himself! Is that
beatitude denied to us, remote as we are in
time and space? How can we, too, gaze upon
that human face, splendid in Him as Son of
Man and Son of God? Perhaps we are like
the disciples on their way to Emmaus, whose
eyes were clouded and who failed to recognize the resurrected Jesus in the pilgrim who
was accompanying them. Or perhaps we must
resign ourselves, in accordance with the tradition attested by, for example, Saint Irenaeus
and Saint Augustine, to confessing that the
mortal appearance of Jesus is completely unknown to us. Great, then, is our good fortune
if the effigy which is alleged to survive on
the sacred Shroud permits us to contemplate
some of the genuine features of the adorable
physical appearance of Our Lord Jesus Christ,
and if in truth it offers relief to our avidity,
so strong today, for visual knowledge of Him!

As we gather around so precious and pious
a relic, His mysterious fascination will grow
in all of us, believers and unbelievers alike,

and in our hearts will resound the evangelical admonition of His voice, which invites us to seek Him where He still is hidden and still can be found, loved and served in human form.

Since the attitude of the church, as expressed through the pope, is significant, it is important here to compare Pope Paul's statement with the attitudes of some of his predecessors. Writing in *Esquire* magazine in 1971, Karl E. Meyer outlined some of the most significant attitudes:

In 1582, Gregory XIII granted a plenary indulgence to all who visited the Shroud when it was exposed in that year; in 1814, when he was returning from the Coronation of Napoleon, and again a year later, when he passed through Turin, Pius VII prostrated himself before the Shroud, and solemnly incensed the relic; new indulgences were granted on successive exhibitions by Gregory XVI, Pius IX and Leo XIII; Pius X enriched the devotion which was attached to the image of the Shroud after 1898; and in 1936, Pius XI, who had scientific training and who took a special interest in the Shroud, gave photographs of the fabric to a group of Catholic Action pilgrims, and spoke these words: "These are pictures which divine Providence has sent precisely for you. . . . They are pictures that come to us from the Holy Shroud of Turin, which is still an object of mystery, but which certainly was not made by human hands, as can now be said to be demonstrated." More recently, John XXIII, after looking at the Shroud's image, was heard to say, "This can only be the Lord's doing!"

By either act or utterance, over thirty popes have contributed to belief in the Shroud's authenticity, although it should be noted that, in the words of Father Rinaldi:

> Its authenticity, like the authenticity of any relic, is not within the scope of the Church's doctrinal definitions. She leaves it to archaeology and other related sciences. A well-established tradition is all the Church requires to permit the cult of a relic. Unless science can clearly disprove a relic's claim to authenticity, the Church will not interfere. We should remember, too, that (as in the case of images and statues) the cult or veneration is directly intended for the person of Christ or of a given saint, and only indirectly for the relic itself.

As the televised exposition of 1973 closed, Cardinal Pellegrino said:

> Let us present ourselves before the dead and living Christ, now and forever, with all the weight of our sufferings, and the sufferings of the poor, the oppressed, the infirm, the underprivileged, in whom the image of Christ is even more vividly reflected: for if it can be doubted, as some do doubt, that the image we piously venerate is really the imprint left by the body of Christ on the new shroud in

which it was wrapped by Joseph of Arimathaea, one thing is beyond doubt, and that
is that the face of Christ is imprinted in that
of his brothers and ours, of those who have,
for all too many selfish and indifferent people, neither faces nor voices. May this hour
of intense emotion not pass in vain; may it
leave in our spirits an ineradicable imprint
of generous acceptance of the Cross and of
effective solidarity with our brothers.

On November 24, 1973, after the televised exposition of the Shroud, the studies that had been
demanded for so long by so many people finally
began. Participating in the tests and examinations
were: Dr. Cesare Codegone, director of the department of technological physics at the Poly-
technic of Turin; Professor Enzo De Lorenzi, head
of the radiological laboratory of the Mauriziano
Hospital of Turin; Dr. Giorgio Frache, director of
the Institute of Legal Medicine, University of Mo-
dena, in collaboration with his colleagues, Dr. Eu-
genia Mari Rizzati and Dr. Emilio Mari; Professor
Guido Filogamo, director of the Institute of Human Anatomy at the University of Turin, in collaboration with his colleague, Alberto Zina; Professor Silvio Curto, curator of the Egyptian Museum
of Turin; and Professor Noemi Gabrielli, retired
director of the art galleries of Piedmont.

Included in the group, but not issuing reports,
were Professor Giovanni Judica-Cordiglia, lecturer
in forensic medicine at Milan University, and
Professor Mario Milone, director of the Institute
of Chemistry at the University of Turin. Acting as
consultants to the commission were Dr. Max Frei,

a Swiss criminologist who specializes in the analysis of microparticles, and Professor G. Raes, a Belgian textile authority.

At the beginning of the studies, twelve threads were excised from the cloth with a fine needle, and two small fragments were cut from it. (On April 10, 1977, *The London Sunday Times* quoted Monsignor Pietro Caramello, the custodian of the Shroud and chairman of the commission, as having denied that the two fragments were removed. Nonetheless Monsignor Caramello signed the commission report in which the removal of the fragments is documented; I, as well as others, have photographs of the fragments and a chart showing their original location on the Shroud, and several scientists have examined them.)

In the report of the commission, published in January 1976, the members issued their individual findings and theories.

Dr. Codegone issued a dissertation on the efficacy of carbon-14 dating of the Shroud, concluding that the process was not sufficiently reliable to justify destruction of the necessary quantity of the fabric. Apparently, he was not aware of progress made in the carbon-14 process that has significantly increased its reliability and significantly decreased the size of the samples needed.

Professor De Lorenzi determined that radiological examination of the Shroud would not provide useful results, a conclusion that has been seriously challenged by other experts, as we shall see in the following chapter. De Lorenzi was somewhat more hopeful about spectrographic examination, but no spectrographic tests were conducted.

Doctors Frache, Rizzati and Mari analyzed five

separate threads extracted from the Shroud in areas where what are believed to be bloodstains are distinctly visible. They were unable to isolate positive traces, but the scientists cautioned against drawing conclusions from such an ancient cloth. They refused to exclude the possibility that blood is present on the samples, but they conducted no tests to identify the stains as anything other than blood.

They did, however, make the most important discovery of the commission: the coloring of the threads and fibers they examined is found only on the surface fibers, with virtually no penetration. If the Shroud is the result of either chemical or artistic treatment, some impregnation of the fabric beyond the surface fibers would seem mandatory.

Professors Filogamo and Zina conducted microscopic examinations of two threads to ascertain if traces of blood could be identified. Although their tests also proved inconclusive, they did discover three distinctly different microscopic granules or globules. The first is of an "indeterminable nature," the second is bacterial spores and the third is "probably of an organic nature."

Professor Curto wrote his dissertation on the nature of the cloth, its weave and its possible origin. Although he would not rule out authenticity, he leaned to a theory of an artistic printing technique using a model or molds. Such a process, most experts believe, could not possibly antedate the tenth century. This theory, however, cannot be reconciled with any of the medical or scientific evidence.

Professor Raes discovered and identified the

traces of cotton fibers already mentioned earlier in this book.

Professor Gabrielli, although stating categorically that microscopic examinations eliminate the possibility of painted Shroud images, proceeded to describe them as some kind of printing or stamping produced by an artist at the end of the fourteenth or at the beginning of the fifteenth century. She also claimed that the Turin Shroud is not the same one owned by the de Charny family as early as 1356. Her explanation of this theory has proved generally unacceptable and seems directly contrary to everything we know about the Shroud.

The report of the commission, so long awaited, proves inconclusive at best, and, in my opinion, naïve and uninformed at worst. A critical study of the report was published by the International Center of Sindonology, which is tantamount to the authority that appointed the commission in the first place. Although specific and complex, the critique, as translated and condensed by Father Rinaldi, makes ten basic points about the commission's work:

1. The composition of the commission was inadequate. Only a few of the disciplines involved in research on the Shroud were represented.

2. The members of the commission, while competent in their particular fields, had never before been exposed to the complexities of the Shroud.

3. The members of the commission did not work in concert with each other. Rather, each came to his or her conclusions independently.

4. In the course of the investigation by the commission, some basic facts were ascertained

and some unexpected findings were made, but the members skirted the issue of authenticity.

5. While chemical analysis of the stains on the Shroud did not isolate blood components, no effort was made by the commission to determine the true nature of the two distinct types of images on the cloth: the tenuous sepia responsible for the negative body images and the darker brown of the stains believed to be blood.

6. The dismissal of the potential importance of radiological, spectrographic and carbon-14 dating was criticized.

7. Having made the unexpected discovery of the superficial nature of the images, the commission did not pursue the discovery and reach a conclusion.

8. There was no report by a forensic scientist.

9. The commission did not examine the reverse side of the Shroud to determine if the totality of the images are as superficial as the samples tested.

10. The commission made no effort to integrate the results of its work with previous findings.

Since the televised exposition and tests of 1973, the attitudes of the Turin authorities toward further exposition and testing of the cloth have improved radically. That they sponsored and published a critique of their own commission's report, admitting its deficiencies, is, in itself, remarkable.

In May 1978—the fourth centennial of the Shroud's arrival in Turin—an International Congress is scheduled to bring together sindonologists from all over the world to conduct the most sophisticated tests that contemporary science can devise. Scheduled for the same time is the first public exposition of the Shroud, since 1933. It is estimated that as many as five million people will make the pilgrimage to view the Shroud.

XIV

The Shroud and Space-Age Science

The Reverend Francis L. Filas, a professor of theology at Loyola University and an indefatigable publicist for the Shroud since 1948, has compared the study of the cloth to study of black holes in the universe. The more we know about it, he says, the more we know we don't know. His comparison is well taken.

Paul Vignon remained until his death a devoted partisan of the authenticity of the Shroud. His second book on the subject, the monumental *Le Saint Suaire de Turin devant la science, l'archéologie, l'histoire, l'iconographie, la logique*, was published in 1938. It was never published in an English translation, even though, while flawed, it is one of the seminal works in the field.

Vignon's vaporograph theory had come under intense criticism, and while he maintained that his thesis had been neither disproved nor replaced with a more substantial one, he was one of his own sternest critics. For example, he pointed out the difficulty in reconciling the notion of a moist cloth clinging to the body, as it must have done to be stained with blood, while at the same time accepting an image so perfect and so subtle in its detail that it would seem the Shroud must have been a perfectly flat surface. In addition, he and several others recognized that the ammoniacal vapors might not have acted as effectively on the aloes-impregnated cloth as he had previously thought. The amount of urea might not have been sufficient, and its transformation through fermentation might have taken too long.

The most severe blow to Vignon's theory came in 1973, when microscopic examinations conducted by the scientific commission indicated that the stains on the cloth are quite superficial, with virtually no impregnation beyond the surface fibers. By whatever name it is called, Vignon's is basically a diffusion theory, involving the transmission of moisture from the body to the cloth. For the theory to be acceptable, it would seem that some penetration of the fabric, at least in the darker areas of the image, through capillary flow or absorption, would be mandatory.

Ray N. Rogers, an archaeologist and thermochemist with the Los Alamos Scientific Laboratory, believes that the fire that damaged the Shroud in 1532 offers substantial proof against Vignon's theory. He says: "I do not see how the image could be a reaction product of ammonia with aloes, because the organic product should be reasonably heat-sensitive."

During the fire, the Shroud was folded in its silver casket. Therefore, different parts of the Shroud were exposed to widely varying temperatures. Rogers continues: "Pure cellulose [a primary constituent of linen] begins to produce gaseous products at an appreciable rate shortly before 590 degrees Fahrenheit [310 degrees Centigrade]; unprocessed cotton batting and newsprint begin to pyrolyze [decompose] rapidly at about 446 degrees Fahrenheit [230 degrees Centigrade]. Parts of the

Shroud were, then, subjected to temperatures sufficient to produce darkening for some unspecified time. Not all of the Shroud was darkened by the fire; therefore, a rather steep thermal gradient had to exist. However, parts of the image that are essentially in contact with darkened areas [caused by the fire] have, as nearly as can be observed, *identical* color tone and density as parts of the image at maximum distance from a discolored area. If large, complicated, natural-product organic molecules were responsible for the image, they should have decomposed, changed color or volatilized at different rates, depending on their distance from a high-temperature zone during the fire. There is no evidence for any variations at all."

Additional evidence against the diffusion theory has been compiled in the form of highly complex probability studies conducted by Dr. Eric Jumper, an aerodynamicist, and Dr. John Jackson, a physicist, both assistant professors at the U.S. Air Force Academy.

(It must be noted here that Rogers, Jumper and Jackson, as well as others who will be quoted in this chapter, are thorough, conscientious, cautious scientists. In all cases, their work is part of ongoing study, and in most cases they do not regard their observations as conclusive—nor should we—until their research has been completed. In addition, all the work herein quoted has been conducted by individuals on their own time at their own initiative. The association of these individuals with certain institutions is for identification purposes only and should imply neither the endorsement nor support of these institutions for their research or theories.

In the past, some scientists, most notably two

experts in forensic medicine, Dr. Giovanni Judica-Cordiglia and Dr. R. Romanese, and the chemist Dr. P. Scotti, were bothered by the idea that vapors transmitted through space were capable of causing anything like the undistorted images of the Shroud. Therefore, they conducted their own research to determine if direct contact between the body and the cloth could have produced stains of such fidelity.

Dr. Judica-Cordiglia moistened a corpse with blood and covered it with a strip of linen soaked in a solution of olive oil and turpentine (certain resinous substances are believed to be part of the mixture with which the Shroud was anointed) mixed with aloes. When he exposed the linen-draped body to hot steam in the presence of light, he was able to produce images with the negative characteristics, if not the perfection, of those on the Shroud.

Dr. Romanese dampened a corpse with a solution of physiological salt, which is found naturally in perspiration, and he sprinkled linen with powdered aloes. When the linen was draped over the corpse and exposed to light, Romanese was also able to produce crude images similar to those of the Shroud.

Dr. Scotti conducted extensive studies into the nature of aloes. As we have already learned, an emulsion of aloes in olive oil yields aloetine. Vignon believed that the presence of ammoniacal vapors was necessary for a reaction with the aloetine that would cause the cloth to brown and thus form images. But Scotti's experiments showed that simple contact with the air could cause the aloetine-soaked cloth to begin to form images. The images are extremely faint at first, but they darken with time. In addition, exposure to sunlight makes the images much more pronounced and their color more vivid.

Scotti's findings have particular appeal for those who are troubled by John's failure to mention the images when the burial clothes were found in Jesus' tomb. If Scotti's theory is correct, they say, the images had not yet formed and did not form until sometime later. Adhering to Scotti's theory, it is reasonable to assume that images might have taken months to form, thus explaining John's silence. But it is unimaginable that such a process took centuries, which some scholars venture is the reason that early claimants to having seen the Shroud did not discern the images.

At any rate, the images produced by Judica-Cordiglia, Romanese and Scotti are only slightly more realistic than those produced by Vignon and are even more open to objections. But today, with our more sophisticated knowledge of the Shroud, the direct-contact theories, like so many other hypotheses, must be regarded largely as matters of historic interest.

In March 1974, the study of the Shroud finally entered the realm of sophisticated, space-age science. Two young physicists—the aforementioned Drs. Jackson and Jumper—were stationed at the Air Force Weapons Laboratory in Albuquerque, New Mexico. The men and their families became friends. After dinner one night, Jackson —who, in addition to his advanced scientific degrees, holds a B.A. in religious studies, and who had already begun some preliminary scientific work on the Shroud with Don Devan, a computer and image-processing specialist—showed Jumper a photograph of the Shroud and related part of its story. Jumper was skeptical but intrigued. He began to read more, and he became hooked.

Jackson and Jumper—along with other scientists they enlisted in their cause—possessed a range of scientific knowledge that no one in the past had even considered as being relevant to Shroud study. They also had access to scientific instruments and techniques, some of which were developed specifically for the U.S. space program, that could do and see things that the human machine cannot.

The team made headlines in November 1976, when a widely published U.P.I. story announced that they had determined, through studies of the Shroud, that Jesus was 5 feet, 10½ inches tall and weighed 175 pounds. As fascinating as the press found this information, it was in fact only preliminary to the most important discoveries that the team has made.

Working with Don Devan, Jackson and Jumper began their work by computer enhancement and computer analysis of Shroud photographs. These are processes used to extract maximum visual information from photographs, particularly those beamed back from various United States space vehicles.

Devan defines enhancement as making an image more suitable for human visualization by "the removal of distracting, noninformative features [generically referred to as "noise"], the sharpening of blurred or indistinct edges or the exaggeration of subtle differences in gray shade or color value." This is accomplished through the use of various filtering methods. Thus, in the case of the Shroud, vague or hazy details of the body images can be amplified, and bothersome visual features such as creases or the texture of the cloth can be suppressed, resulting in new photographs that are easier to study visually and may yield more information.

Image analysis, a more complex process, provides a mathematical measurement of image properties. The eye can distinguish between sharp or blurred edges and between rough or smooth textures. But image analysis can calculate a precise measurement of exactly how sharp or exactly how rough. This allows a definitive comparison of image areas, resulting in an accurate evaluation of the image properties.

The team used a computer to transform the visual information contained in the gray shades of the Shroud photographs into a set of numerical values. The numerical representation of the photographs was processed by a computer and a new computer-enhanced image was re-created on a viewing screen. On one of the computer-enhanced photographs, faint images that are not visible on the original photographs appeared alongside the knees. The team concluded that "these images were side images of the legs and not just an anomaly of the particular photograph scanned, burn mark or water stain resulting from extinguishing the fire of 1532. The existence of these side images is significant because it suggests that the image-forming process on the Shroud had to be a horizontal as well as a vertical one."

Realizing that this discovery indicates that encoded in the varying intensity levels of the Shroud image is actual three-dimensional information which defines the contours of Jesus' body, Jackson and Jumper proceeded to research this three-dimensional quality in depth.

To avoid any chance of misinterpreting or misrepresenting this important work, I quote directly and at length from their paper entitled "The Three-Dimension Image on Jesus' Burial Cloth," written with Bill Mottern and edited by Kenneth E. Stevenson:

> Vignon noted that the intensity of the image seemed to vary inversely with cloth-body distance. Unlike Vignon, however, we have highly sensitive image-recording equipment that allowed us to test his hypothesis. We also feel that our research sheds new light on the uniformity of the process that formed the image on the Shroud and on the Shroud's authenticity. Our approach consists of three parts: (1) measurement of cloth-body distance; (2) measurement of image intensity; (3) comparison of cloth-body distance with image intensity at various locations on the Shroud.
>
> To measure cloth-body distance, we had to reconstruct Jesus' burial configuration. We accomplished this by covering a volunteer subject of proper height and proportions with a cloth model of the Shroud. Correct draping of the cloth was the most important aspect of this stage, since we had to ensure that all image features (which we traced to scale from a projection of a photograph of the Shroud onto the cloth) were positioned over the corresponding body part. Photographs of this reconfiguration, with and without the cloth in place, allowed us to measure

perpendicular cloth-body distance from the ridge line of the cloth.

To accomplish the next step, measurement of image intensity, we used a microdensitometer to scan the image on the Shroud along the path of the ridge line. (The ridge line indicates the body's highest points of contact with the Shroud.) This step allowed us to correlate measured image intensity with cloth-body distance at known points on the Shroud, in this case along the well-defined ridge line. We were then able to correlate a plot of image intensity with cloth-body distance and establish the relationship between the two.

Once we established the correlation between cloth-body distance and image intensity, it became apparent that the image on the Shroud might be equivalent to a three-dimensional surface of Jesus' body. In fact, the microdensitometer plot of image intensity alone provides a distorted profile of Jesus' body! Using our experimentally determined cloth-body distance data in conjunction with image intensity, we were able to remove much of the distortion. The only remaining step was to mathematically construct a fully three-dimensional surface image of the Man of the Shroud.

At the suggestion of Bill Mottern, we converted all image points to correct vertical relief rather than just those image points of the ridge line. Using Interpretation System's VP-8 Image Analyzer, a device that plots shades of image intensity as adjustable levels of vertical relief, we were able to form a three-dimensional brightness surface of the Shroud image. The wide versatility of this instrument also allowed us to test varying amounts of relief (which helped to approximate our experimental fall-off curve), as well as to rotate the resulting image and thereby view it from various angles. Plate 25 shows a computer-generated relief surface of the entire body image, front (left) and back (right).

In perspective, a three-dimensional image of the Shroud is not as insignificant as it might seem. However, ordinary photographic images cannot usually be converted to true three-dimensional replicas. The photographic process does not cause the objects filmed to become exposed in direct relationship to distance from the camera. Only when the degree of illumination received from an object depends, in some way, upon its distance (for example, in a stellar photograph) would three-dimensional analysis and reconstruction be possible. Otherwise, no less than two photographs (as in stereo photography) separated by a known distance are required to produce a true relief image. Ordinary photographs of persons transformed into vertical relief showed obvious distortion; noses were pushed into faces, arms into chests and entire reliefs appeared flat and unnatural.

Since the body form is natural, proportioned and lacks any apparent distortion, it would seem clear that: (1) the image formation was uniform and independent of body surface qualities; (2) the lay of the Shroud was relatively flat; (3) processes [random chemical or bacterial degradation] tending to change image intensity acted uniformly or not at all. Since no distortion exists when the Shroud image is transformed, its three-dimensionality must be a distinctive characteristic. Also, it is possible to conclude that the Shroud was not produced by direct contact where discoloration of the cloth occurred, only where the Shroud touched the body. Direct contact would cause the image to appear flat-topped, with all areas of contact having the same vertical elevation. For the same reason, artistic production of the Shroud must be ruled unlikely. In fact, two expert artists' reproductions of the Shroud failed to produce the excellent three-dimensional image relief of the Shroud itself.

Another photograph of the Shroud that we subjected to relief enhancement was a close-up of the face. As you can see in Plate 24, the process revealed something unexpected —over each eye appeared objects resembling small buttons. Our research left us with but one conclusion—the button-like features are what they seem to be, namely solid objects resting upon the eyelids. This identification agrees with ancient Jewish burial customs, in which objects [potsherd fragments or coins] were sometimes placed over the eyes. Detailed identification is not possible without further investigation, but we propose that they may be some kind of coinage since: (1) they are both nearly circular and they approximate the same size such as were coins [in fact, Ian Wilson has documented a coin minted in A.D. 30 or 31 that is of correspondent size and bears the image of Pontius

Pilate]; (2) Joseph of Arimathea, a wealthy man, was responsible for burying Jesus. Thus, if Joseph followed the burial custom to cover the eyes, then it is not unreasonable that the most convenient and natural thing for him to use would have been coins. If the items prove to be coins, then we may have a truly unique method of dating the image. Also, the image-making process must have acted through space, independent of the body and any chemicals present, for it acted on these buttons. . . .

Jackson would later equate his reaction to the first sight of the undistorted three-dimensional image with that of Secondo Pia, when, alone in his darkroom, he discovered the negativity of the Shroud image. And justifiably so, for the ancient strip of linen had yielded its most tantalizing information to date: encoded in its varying levels of image intensity—the intensities that formed the subtle shadings of the Shroud picture—was a virtually perfect three-dimensional portrait of the Man of the Shroud. And neither camera nor artist could have produced the portrait, in this year or in any other, certainly not prior to the fourteenth century. And it is essential to note that the portrait could be detected only by today's most sophisticated computer hardware.

The computer had yielded other startling information, too—circular, uniform bulges on both eyes. It is inconceivable that an artist could have painted so perfectly what neither his nor any other eyes could see. But for those who still cling to theories of artistic reproduction, we turn again to archaeologist and thermochemist Ray Rogers:

If the image were painted, it had to be painted with a colored material; otherwise, the artist could not observe the progress of his work. What colored materials could have been used prior to the known history of the Shroud? Most would have been inorganic in an organic vehicle or water, *e.g.*, ocher in oil or egg white. More unlikely would have been natural organic pigments or stains; however, many of them would have been plant or animal porphyrins, all of which contain characteristic metals. Purely organic materials can be rejected on obvious grounds. Purely inorganic pigments may not have been changed by the heating received at the time of the fire, but all organic colors should have suffered a change in proportion to the severity of the heating they received. The closer the organic vehicle or dye to a heated area, the greater should be its change of color or density. No variation of color with position is observed on the Shroud: shading is accomplished by variation of density, not color. Tone remains constant with position. I believe that the obvious thermal gradient that existed at the time of the fire eliminates the possibility that any organic vehicle was used for an inorganic pigment, that any organic pigment, dye or stain was used, or that any common porphyrin pigment was used. The lack of observed capillary flow or absorption seems to eliminate most water-based [ink-like] inorganic systems from consideration. . . .

I also cannot see any evidence for migration of any of the image as a result of water percolation. If soluble pigments had been used, they would have moved. Many insoluble pigments would have produced soluble products as a result of the heat and reactive pyrolysis products of the cloth. . . .

The only conclusion that can be reached is that, if the image were painted, a stable, particulate inorganic pigment in a water base had to have been used. . . .

I believe that the best way to test nondestructively for the presence or absence of inorganic pigments would be by X-ray fluorescence, and I consider this analysis to be the most important nondestructive test that can be run during the 1978 viewing.

Donald J. Lynn is with the Image Processing Laboratory of the Jet Propulsion Laboratory, California Institute of Technology. He directed I.P.L.'s activities in support of the Mariner 10 flyby of Venus and Mercury and the highly successful Viking mission to Mars. Together with Jean J. Lorre, also an image processing analyst with the Jet Propulsion Laboratory, who has worked on many of the photographs beamed back by various space probes, Lynn began in 1976 computer enhancement of Shroud photographs in an effort to discover more details and eliminate the "noise" earlier referred to by Don Devan. Although Lynn and Lorre found the photographs of insufficient resolution and quality to go much beyond what had already been found, their work did produce sophisticated scientific support for several longbelieved theories:

1. The water marks and the numerous small intense features on the body have abrupt

edges, whereas the large burn marks have smoothly decaying edges. This suggests a different mechanism of formation for the two types of features.

2. The short, linear marks with small spots along them, which appear on the back of the figure, could be attributed to scourge marks. These marks seem to be separable into two different, predominantly diagonal directions [indicating that two men carried out the flogging].

3. The image of the facial region is composed of a wide range of spatial frequencies that are oriented in a random fashion. This indicates that the feature-generating mechanism was probably directionless [a characteristic that would not be consistent with hand application thus providing additional evidence that the image was not painted].

Dr. Max Frei, as mentioned in the preceding chapter, is a Swiss criminologist who specializes in the analysis of microparticles. He was also a consultant to the 1973 scientific commission. During his proximity to the cloth, he made scrapings from the Shroud, which he then analyzed. Although Dr. Frei wishes to maintain a proprietary interest in his complete findings until he presents them at the International Congress on the Shroud in 1978, he has issued the following statement: "I can state with certainty that the Turin Shroud dates from the time of Christ." The particles he studied reveal, he says, the presence of certain pollen fossils that "could only have originated from plants that grew exclusively in Palestine at the time of Christ." Frei has further indicated that other fossilized pollens can document the Shroud's existence in Turkey, France and Italy. Palestine . . . Edessa . . . France . . . Italy—this is the exact itinerary that the Shroud of Turin must have if it is authentic and if its now speculative history is accurate.

We await confirmation of Frei's evidence from other experts. I have reservations about his findings because pollen is known to travel almost incredible distances by any number of means. In addition, until all the extraneous elements on or trapped in the weave of the Shroud are isolated and identified, I do not see how contamination can be discounted.

Throughout this book, we have so far explored the Shroud within the bounds of natural laws, scientifically acceptable premises and accountable phenomena. Remaining within these limits, we have dealt with Jesus only as a historical personage and have cautiously accepted the Gospel accounts of the Passion as being basically factual. Such explanations should be acceptable to Jew or Christian, atheist or agnostic. But we have also found that in light of recent evidence, neither the vaporograph nor the direct-contact theories offers acceptable explanations of the cause of the body images on the Shroud. It is here that we must confront the possibility of Jesus' resurrection, and the effect it might have had on the Shroud.

In 1966, bothered that none of the prevailing explanations of the body images seemed definitive, Geoffrey Ashe, a British scholar, began experimenting with the production of images on linen through heat radiation. Using a heated brass ornament on which there was a horse in relief, he found that if he placed linen over the horse, a clear negative image was formed by a combination of direct contact and heat radiation. The results were far more impressive in their affinity to the images on the Shroud than those produced by any of the other experiments.

Writing in *Sindon*, a periodical devoted exclusively to research into the Shroud and distributed selectively to sindonologists throughout the world, Ashe said:

> The Shroud is explicable if it once enwrapped a human body to which something extraordinary happened. It is not explicable otherwise. The Christian Creed has always affirmed that Our Lord underwent an unparalleled transformation in the tomb. His case is exceptional and perhaps here is the key. It is at least intelligible (and has been suggested several times) that the physical change of the body at the Resurrection may have released a brief and violent burst of some other radiation than heat, perhaps scientifically identifiable, perhaps not, which scorched the cloth. In this case the Shroud image is a quasi-photograph of Christ returning to life, produced by a kind of radiance or "incandescence" partially analogous to heat in its effects. . . . Also, the fact that the bloodstains on the Shroud are positive is now readily accounted for. The blood was matter which had ceased to be part of the body, underwent no change at the Resurrection, and therefore did not scorch, but marked the cloth differently.

Dr. David Willis, a British physician and noted sindonologist, has said of the Ashe theory:

> Perhaps, in our present state of knowledge, that is as good an explanation as any. It is consistent with the present conception of matter as forms of energy and the fact of radiation images formed on stone following the dropping of the atomic bomb at Hiroshima. It also ties in with Leo Vala's conviction that the Shroud image is in some way "photographic." Vala is a brilliant, inventive photographer. As an agnostic his conviction is impressive: "I can prove conclusively that claims calling the Shroud a fake are completely untrue. Even with today's highly advanced photographic resources nobody alive could produce the image—a photographic negative—embodied in the Shroud."

As can be determined from his reserved tone, Geoffrey Ashe is not a religious hysteric. He is a Christian, and any immediate acceptance of his proposal, given the extent of today's scientific knowledge, seems to require an unwavering belief in the Resurrection. It also defines the Shroud as having been subject to supernatural intervention—a miracle—or at least some kind of paranormal occurrence. For some people, such faith is an integral part of their religious lives, and for them, Ashe's hypothesis may be the most palatable theory of all.

But what of the atheist and the agnostic, who, while accepting the historicity of Jesus, reject the notion of Resurrection as but another apocryphal story put forth by the disciples to further the spread of Christianity? Must they also dismiss out of hand the possibility of radiation-caused images?

Possibly not, for the idea of body-energy emissions has become, in recent years, a subject of much interest and study, if of only limited scientific acceptance. Alleged evidence of these emissions includes everything from so-called Kirlian photography—the recording on film of images of objects supposedly produced by energy discharge —to experiments with psychics and "healers" who seem capable of emitting some kind of energy, which may be either the cause or effect of whatever extraordinary faculties they possess. No evidence so far indicates that this energy could produce anything like the images on the Shroud. But if there is any validity to these experiments, we may at least have to consider energy discharge —resurrection or no—as a possible cause of the images on the Shroud.

Scientists are cautious when even theoretically discussing the subject, lest their theorizing be misconstrued as support for untested hypotheses of the most sensational impact. It seems evident, however, that if the images were caused by some kind of energy discharge, it would have to be of a type referred to as flash photolysis—a burst of extremely high-intensity heat or light for an extremely short duration, probably registered in milliseconds. Otherwise, there is no way that the resulting "scorch-picture" could fail to penetrate and probably eradicate the cloth or produce an image that would be anything more than an indistinguishable smear.

However the images were formed, we must understand that at this point we are not so much dealing with the actual cause as with individual perceptions of it, based largely on speculative experiments rather than direct evidence. A complete and thorough physical testing of the Shroud may reveal enough clues so that a satisfactory conclusion may be set forth in the future. But until then, no plausible theory can be completely dismissed, and even the most farfetched must be considered. As is becoming more and more obvious, and as Geoffrey Ashe so eloquently and directly put it, "The Shroud is explicable if it once enwrapped a human body to which something extraordinary happened. It is not explicable otherwise."

XV

The New Tests

John Dart, a religion writer for the *Los Angeles Times*, reported: "By any measure, it was an unusual gathering that ended here Thursday [in Albuquerque, New Mexico, March 24, 1977].

"Among the forty participants were scientists from Pasadena's Jet Propulsion Laboratory, the Air Force Academy and nearby Los Alamos Scientific Laboratory; a scientist whose company proved the so-called Vinland map a fake; an eminent British New Testament scholar-theologian; Catholic priests from New York and the Vatican; and four long-haired members of the communal Christ Brotherhood, who just happened to drop by."

It was the 1977 United States Conference of Research on The Shroud of Turin, organized primarily by Dr. John Jackson and Dr. Eric Jumper, acting in conjunction with the Holy Shroud Guild, to bring together Shroud researchers of many disciplines, scientific and scholarly, secular and religious. I was among them. The purpose of the conference was twofold: to share the results of previous work, and to formulate recommendations to be presented to the Turin authorities for a series of tests—more informed and sophisticated than any yet performed—to be conducted in the United

States and in Turin before and during the International Congress on the Shroud scheduled for May 1978.

The issue of these tests, as may be assumed from the attitudes of the Turin authorities in past years, is complex. There are Shroud research groups in many countries, all vying to test their own theories. There will undoubtedly be, as has been the case in the past, limited time available for those tests. And with the possible exception of the threads and fabric samples already excised from the cloth, all tests must be nondestructive.

The point of greatest significance is that there is still much information that the Shroud can yield. The secrets it retains are probably far greater than the knowledge we now have, and all hopes of complete authentication or complete refutation of authenticity rest on these tests.

Interdisciplinary coordination among the groups recommending tests is mandatory, the equipment used must be the most sensitive available, the methodology must be sound and the technological authority of those designated to do the work must be beyond reproach. The time has long since passed when scientific work on the Shroud is so subject to reproach that it is invalidated immediately after experiments are conducted.

The combined skills of the proposed American group far exceed the necessary requirements, and, in fact, some of the equipment and several of the processes that can prove most useful are available only in the United States. The following tests and personnel proposed by the American group should yield the ultimate in accurate, meaningful information.

CARBON-14 DATING

For years, the idea of carbon-14 dating of the Shroud has been discussed, debated and, eventually, discarded. The arguments against it have been that it is not yet accurate enough to date an artifact less than two thousand years old and that it is a destructive test, requiring too large a sample of cloth.

All organic materials—plant or animal—absorb carbon-14 from the atmosphere until death, at which time the amount of carbon-14 begins to decay at a fixed rate. By establishing scales based on the rate of decay of carbon-14 in organic materials of a known age, and then by finding the rate of decay in materials of an age unknown, comparisons can be made and the latter dated. But to count the amount of decayed carbon-14, samples of the material must be destroyed.

According to Dr. Walter C. McCrone, the process has now become sophisticated enough to date a two-thousand-year-old artifact with an accepted accuracy of plus or minus fifty years. At this writing, one count will require a linen sample weighing no more than sixty milligrams and being no larger than three square centimeters, and advances in the field of carbon-dating are being made so rapidly that even this size requirement should be significantly reduced in coming months. All contamination can be successfully removed. The more samples that can be counted, the greater the accuracy. One of the samples excised from the Shroud in 1973 meets the minimum weight and size, and a second sample is twice the minimum requirements. Thus, three counts are feasible, with no further destruction of the cloth. And in the case of the Shroud, an accuracy of plus or minus fifty years would be virtually conclusive, certainly to the extent of eliminating fraud.

Dr. McCrone is president of Walter C. McCrone Associates, Inc., a Chicago laboratory specializing in the analysis of microparticles. The McCrone laboratory achieved instant recognition when it successfully proved that the Vinland Map (which purported to show North America as discovered by Leif Ericson, thus predating Columbus) was a fake. The lab also does extensive criminology and environment studies and is one of the best-equipped facilities in the world. It is under the supervision of Dr. McCrone that the carbon-14 dating process would, it is hoped, be carried out.

Ion Microprobe Analysis

The ion microprobe (of which fewer than twenty exist in the world, all in the United States) is one of the most sensitive microdetection tools yet developed. It can identify traces of all 104 elements in the periodic table from a sample ten times smaller than the human eye can see.

Through ion microprobe analysis—and possibly other microscopic processes such as microramen spectroscopy and ESCA (electron spectroscopy for chemical analysis), which, although extremely complex, essentially yield microparticle identification of natural and extraneous substances—many of the mysteries of the Shroud can potentially be solved.

We know the chemical composition of the body and its fluids; we know the composition of blood;

we know what fire or radiation or chemicals or pigments can do to cloth. And once we know what traces of what elements in what quantities and in what distribution have been left on the Shroud of Turin, we should be able to determine whether it contained a human body, where it has been and even how its images were formed.

Dr. McCrone's laboratory has already been able to determine the authenticity of Persian burial silks from the twelfth century, identifying both blood and other body fluids, as well as establishing that different samples came from the same burial site. The Shroud will probably prove more difficult to test, but then no one has yet "looked" —using those instruments that can "see"—who knew what he was looking for.

INFRARED ANALYSIS, X-RAY FLUORESCENCE AND RADIOGRAPHIC ANALYSIS

Roger Morris of Los Alamos Scientific Laboratory, Bill Mottern of Sandia Laboratories and Joseph Accetta of the Air Force Weapons Laboratory have been designated as the members of the American scientific team that would conduct infrared analysis, X-ray fluorescence and radiographic analysis of the Shroud. They are all physicists, with forty years' experience among them in state-of-the-art technology. Speaking for the team, Joe Accetta has outlined the nature of the tests and what they may detect:

The space around us is full of radiation, most of it harmless and invisible, but nevertheless capable of being detected. Some familiar examples are X rays, visible rays, radio waves and heat or infrared rays. The only real distinction between these waves or rays are their relative energies. Some of this radiation can be detected by the human body; for example, the eye is sensitive to light or visible rays and the skin is sensitive to some heat rays. It turns out that the other regions within the total electromagnetic spectrum can yield a wealth of information about something if one has the appropriate devices to sense and record it. Much of the work proposed herein will be an investigation of these "other" regions and the extraction of information from them.

In the infrared analysis experiment, we propose to examine regions of the spectrum that lie below the visible in energy. One can create an image of an object in the infrared region in much the same fashion as the eye creates an image in the visible [region]. These images are called thermograms, or heat pictures. In addition, there is film that is sensitive to the most energetic regions of the infrared. We propose to utilize both of these techniques to search for additional details that are not visible to the eye. Images of common objects appear vastly different in the infrared because the minute differences in contrast from point to point that create an image are caused by changes in temperature rather than changes in reflectance, as in the case of conventional photography.

A second aspect of the infrared work is that substances can sometimes be identified by measuring the relative amounts of radiation present in a series of narrow energy regions in the infrared. This technique forms a characteristic spectrum that is sometimes unique to a specific material or substance. By measuring this "signature" we hope to identify one or more substances that might be responsible for the image.

Much of the previous discussion is applicable to [X-ray fluorescence analysis]. Only this time we examine a region that is considerably above the visible in terms of energy. When materials are bombarded with X rays of selected energy, they in turn re-emit a characteristic set or spectrum of other X rays. The amounts and energies of the emitted X rays are unique to a given element. By examining the re-emitted X rays, we hope to identify specific elements present in the Shroud. [Ray Rogers believes that this test will be the most useful in determining the presence or absence of inorganic pigments and thus finally confirm or dispel any ideas of an artistic process. In addition, the distribution of elements across the Shroud and its images is of considerable importance in determining if it did contain a human body. Sodium or chlorine deposits from body fluids, traces of iron from blood—all should be detectable by this process.]

[Radiographic Analysis] is a technique that everyone is familiar with. In this experiment, the Shroud will be subjected to a harmless bombardment of soft or low-energy X rays in much the same fashion as a medical X ray. The resulting image will be recorded on special film placed behind the Shroud. These images are created by a variation in density from point to point on the object. The experiment may yield more details of the image and perhaps areas of high metal concentration. It will also yield clues as to which areas of the Shroud might be fruitful for further investigation using other techniques.

NEW SCIENTIFIC PHOTOGRAPHS

It is not to denigrate the accomplishments or equipment of previous Shroud photographers that I state there is little more to be gleaned from existing photographs. The fact is that, at the advanced state of present technology, the human eye is one of the most limited visual instruments we have. This point can be dramatized by a discussion that took place at the Albuquerque conference.

Everyone present who had ever seen the Shroud —not just photographs of it—saw two distinctly different colors: the faint sepia of the body images and the dark brown of the bloodstains. Yet when color photographs of the Shroud are subjected to computer scanning equipment, it turns out that there is really only one color—of widely varying intensities. All existing photographs were taken to be viewed by the unaided eye. In fact, great effort has gone into notarizing that they are true to the original and that no effort was made to obtain anything but visual fidelity.

If the American image-enhancement and analysis team—composed of Don Lynn and Jean Lorre of the Jet Propulsion Laboratory, Don Devan of Information Science, Inc., Don Janney of

Los Alamos Scientific Laboratory and Bill Mottern of Sandia Laboratory—is to provide any more information about the Shroud with its highly sophisticated scanning equipment, it now needs a series of photographs taken specifically for analysis by its machinery. The photographer of the American group is Charles Webb, a scientific photographer with over fifteen years' experience. His position with Eastman Kodak's Colorado division and his association with image-enhancement specialists puts him in a unique position to see that the latest, most sophisticated equipment and processes are used.

High-resolution photography of some areas should provide a wealth of new information. For example, Dr. Jackson and Dr. Jumper have already alluded to the bulges over the eyes that they have discovered. Existing photographs, however, yield nothing but vague outlines. High-resolution photography of the eyes might well permit concrete identification of these bulges.

Various filtering techniques will aid photographers in freeing their photographs from "noise" and unwanted information. For example, the weave texture of the cloth may be eliminated so the actual images can be studied more carefully. Other processes will sharpen hazy areas for better identification.

A new series of photographs might enable image analysts to determine what image areas were formed by particular physical processes (if, for instance, the bloodstained regions were formed by the same process that produced the body images), and whether textural distinctions between hair, beard and flesh regions are consistent with true characteristics. If they are not consistent, some type of imprinting would be implied.

As is evident, some of the new tests proposed here can produce multidiscipline confirmation of the same information. Considering the questions the Shroud still poses and the degree to which its authenticity is still dismissed out of hand, these information overlaps must not be regarded—either by the Turin authorities or by the general public —as repetitious. Rather, they are absolutely necessary, as are any other nondestructive experiments that can shed additional light on the ancient cloth.

XVI

Conclusion

There is not now a satisfactory conclusion to the story of the Shroud of Turin. There will be none until authenticity is confirmed or denied. Although the results of—indeed, the authorization to proceed with—the new round of tests are being awaited with great optimism, there may never be sufficient data for categorical proofs. Nonetheless, even the most skeptical no longer rush to deny the validity of the Shroud. Rather, they maintain relative silence. Those who do attempt to explain it away are largely uninformed and are quickly trounced by the massive weight of scientific and scholarly evidence already compiled. Some arguments do live on, but they are basically restricted to rather esoteric points which, while not unimportant, will not significantly affect the final judgment.

But even if tests prove the Shroud is not a fraud, even if it can be conclusively shown that the images of the body were not put there by artifice, even if the bloodstains are genuine, even if it can be demonstrated that the images are the result of a paranormal occurrence, there will be reasonable people who will swear that there is still no way to prove that the imprint of the Man on the Shroud is of Jesus. The point cannot be easily dismissed, but in the recorded history of the world, only one man has ever been subjected to the unique combination of tortures proclaimed by the Gospels and evident on the Shroud. That man was Jesus Christ. And, in the end, the ancient cloth of Turin may have to be accepted with the same faith on which the whole of Christianity is based.

Bibliography

Accetta, Joseph S. "X-Ray Fluorescence Analysis and Infrared Thermography with Applications to the Shroud of Turin." *Proceedings of the 1977 United States Conference of Research on the Shroud of Turin.* Colorado Springs, 1977, pp. 110–23.

———. Personal communication. May 16, 1977.

Arndt, W.F., and Gingrich, F. Wilbur. *A Greek-English Lexicon of the New Testament and Other Early Christian Literature.* Cambridge, 1952.

Ashe, Geoffrey. "What Sort of Picture?" *Sindon* (1966): pp. 15–19.

Barbet, Pierre. *A Doctor at Calvary.* Translated by the Earl of Wicklow. New York, 1953.

Barnes, Arthur S. *The Holy Shroud of Turin.* London, 1934.

Bender, A.P. "Beliefs, Rites and Customs of the Jews Connected with Death, Burial and Mourning." *Jewish Quarterly Review,* vol. 7 (1894–95): Part 4: pp. 101–18; Part 5: pp. 254–69.

Buchler, A. "L'enterrement des criminels d'après le Talmud et le Midrasch." *Revue des Etudes Juives,* vol. 46 (1903): pp. 74–88.

Bucklin, Robert. "The Legal and Medical Aspects of the Trial and Death of Christ." *Medicine, Science and the Law,* January 1970, pp. 14–26.

Bulst, Werner. *The Shroud of Turin.* Translated by S. McKenna and J.J. Galvin. Milwaukee, 1957.

Catholic Encyclopaedia. New York, 1912. S.v. "Shroud, The Holy."

Cheshire, Leonard. *Pilgrimage to the Shroud.* New York, 1956.

Chevalier, U. *Autour des origines du suaire de Lirey. Avec documents inédits.* Paris, 1903.

――――. *Etude critique sur l'origine du Saint Suaire de Lirey-Chambéry-Turin.* Paris, 1900.

――――. *Le Saint Suaire de Lirey-Chambéry-Turin et les défenseurs son authenticité.* Paris, 1902.

――――. "*Le Saint Suaire de Turin, est-il l'original ou une copie? Etude critique.*" *Mémoires et documents publiés par la société savoisienne d'histoire et d'archéologie*, 2nd series, 13 (1899): pp. 105–33.

――――. "*Le Saint Suaire de Turin et le nouveau testament.*" *Revue Biblique*, vol. 11 (1902): pp. 564–73.

Chifflet, J.J. *De linteis sepulchralibus Christi crisis historica.* Antwerp, 1624.

Daremberg, C., and Saglio, E., eds. *Dictionnaire des antiquités.* Paris, 1896. S.vv. "Crux" and "Flagellum."

Dart, John. "Christian Relic Under Gaze of Science." *Los Angeles Times.* March 25, 1977.

De Clari, Robert. *La conquête de Constantinople.* Edited by P. Lauer. Paris, 1924.

Delage, Yves. "*Le linceul de Turin.*" *Revue Scientifique,* vol. 17 (1902): pp. 683–87.

Devan, Don. Photography of the Turin Shroud for Use in Image Analysis Experiments. *Proceedings of the 1977 United States Conference of Research on the Shroud of Turin.* Colorado Springs, 1977, pp. 136–45.

――――. Personal communication. May 23, 1977.

Dinegar, Robert. "Pastoral Aspects of Scientific Research on the Shroud of Turin." *Proceedings of the 1977 United States Conference of Research on the Shroud of Turin.* Colorado Springs, 1977, pp. 20–22.

Enciclopedia Cattolica. Vatican City, 1948.

Encyclopaedia Judaica. Jerusalem, 1971. S.v. "Burial."

Enrie, Giuseppe. *La Santa Sindone rivelata dalla fotografia.* Turin, 1938.

Epstein, I., ed. *The Babylonian Talmud.* London, 1935–52.

Filas, Francis L. "Ideal Attitudes Concerning Research of the Shroud." *Proceedings of the 1977 United States Conference of Research on the Shroud of Turin.* Colorado Springs, 1977, pp. 13–15.

Fossati, L. *Conversazioni e discussioni sulla santa sindone.* Turin, 1968.

————. *La Santa sindone: nuova luce su antichi documenti.* Turin, 1961.

Geyer, Paulus, ed. *Itinera Hierosolymitana saeculi,* vols. 3–8. Prague, Vienna, Leipzig, 1878.

Graffin, R., and Nau, F., eds. *Patrologia Orientalis.* Paris, 1904–.

Green, Maurus. "Enshrouded in Silence." *Ampleforth Journal,* vol. 74 (1969): pp. 319–45.

Haas, N. "Anthropological Observations on the Skeletal Remains from Giv'at ha-Mivtar." *Israel Exploration Journal,* vol. 20 (1970): pp. 38–59.

Holzmeister, U. *"Crux Domini eiusque crufixio ex archaeologia romana illustrantur." Verbum Domini,* vol. 14 (1934): pp. 149–55, 216–20, 241–49, 257–63.

The Interpreter's Dictionary of the Bible. New York and Nashville, 1962. S.vv. "Bier," "Burial," "Embalming," "Spice."

Jackson, John P. "The Shroud Image Color Analysis and Information *Theory." Proceedings of the 1977 Conference of Research on the Shroud of Turin.* Colorado Springs, 1977, pp. 190–96.

————. Personal communication. January 5, 1977.

Jackson, John P., and Jumper, Eric J., with Mottern, Bill. Kenneth Stevenson, ed. "The Three-Dimensional Image on Jesus' Burial Cloth. *Proceedings of the 1977 United States Conference of Research on the Shroud of Turin.* Colorado Springs, 1977.

Jackson, John P., Jumper, Eric J. and Devan, Don. "Investigations of the Shroud of Turin by Computer-Aided Analysis." *Proceedings of the 1977 United States Conference of Research on the Shroud of Turin.* Colorado Springs, 1977, pp. 74–94.

Janney, Donald H. "Computer-Aided Image Enhancement and Analysis." *Proceedings of the 1977 United States Conference of Research on the Shroud of Turin.* Colorado Springs, 1977, pp. 146–53.

The Jewish Encyclopaedia. New York and London, 1902.

Judica-Cordiglia, G. "*La sepoltura di Gesù e la sacra sindone.*" *Salesianum,* vol. 16 (1954): pp. 153–67.

Jumper, Eric J. "Considerations of Molecular Diffusion and Radiation as an Image-Formation Process on the Shroud." *Proceedings of the 1977 United States Conference of Research on the Shroud of Turin.* Colorado Springs, 1977, pp. 182–89.

————. Personal communication. June 2, 1977.

Klauser, T., ed. *Reallexikon fuer Antike und Christentum.* Stuttgart, 1950–. S.vv. "Christusbild" and "Archeiropoieta."

Lorre, Jean J., and Lynn, Donald J. "Digital Enhancement of Images of the Shroud of Turin." *Proceedings of the 1977 United States Conference of Research on the Shroud of Turin.* Colorado Springs, 1977, pp. 154–81.

Lynn, Donald J. Personal communication. May 24, 1977.

McCown, Thomas M. "Cloth-Body Distance of the Holy Shroud." *Proceedings of the 1977 United States Conference on the Shroud of Turin.* Colorado Springs, 1977, pp. 95–109.

McCrone, Walter C. "Authentication of the Turin Shroud." *Proceedings of the 1977 United States Conference of Research on the Shroud of Turin.* Colorado Springs, 1977, pp. 124–30.

————. Personal communication. June 1977.

Meyer, Karl E. "Were You There When They Photographed My Lord?" *Esquire,* August 1971.

Michelant, H., and Raynaut, G., eds. *Itinéraires à Jérusalem.* Geneva, 1882.

Migne J. L., ed. *Patrologiae Cursus Completus. Series Graeca.* Paris, 1857–66.

————. *Patrologiae Cursus Completus. Series Latina.* Paris, 1844–64.

Mommsen, T. *Roemisches Strafrecht.* Leipzig, 1899.

Moulton, J. H., and Milligan, G. *The Vocabulary of the Greek New Testament Illustrated from the Papyri and Other Non-Literary Sources.* London, 1942.

Naveh, J. "The Ossuary Inscriptions from Giv'at ha-Mivtar." *Israel Exploration Journal,* vol. 20 (1970): pp. 33–37.

The New Catholic Encyclopedia. New York, 1967.

The New English Bible. New York, 1971.

Otterbein, Adam J. "The Holy Shroud." *The New Catholic Encyclopedia,* vol. 13. New York, 1967.

————. "Introduction to the Shroud and State of the Question." *Proceedings of the 1977 United States Conference of Research on the Shroud of Turin.* Colorado Springs, 1977, pp. 1–9.

Pauly, A., Wissowa, G. and Kroll, W., eds. *Real-Encyclopaedie der klassischen Altertumswissenschaft.* Stuttgart, 1893–. S.v. "Crux" by R. Hitzig.

Paterson, Thomas. Personal communication. May 1977.

Report of the Turin Commission on the Holy Shroud. London, 1976.

Riant, P. *Des dépouilles religieuses enlevées à Constantinople au XIIIe siècle par les Latins.* Paris, 1875.

————. *Extrait des mémoires de la société nationale des antiquaires de France,* vol. 36.

Riant, P., ed. *Alexii I Comneni ad Robertum Flandrensem Epistola Spuria.* Geneva, 1877.

————. *Exuviae Sacrae Constantinopolitanae,* vols. 1 and 2. Geneva, 1877–78.

Ricci, Giulio. *La morte di Cristo contestata in nome della santa sindone.* Assisi, 1970.

————. *L'uomo della sindone e Gesù.* Rome, 1969.

————. *Statura dell'uomo della sindone.* Assisi, 1957.

————. "Historical, Medical and Physical Study of the Holy Shroud." *Proceedings of the 1977 United States Conference of Research on the Shroud of Turin.* Colorado Springs, 1977, pp. 58–73.

Rinaldi, Peter M. *It Is the Lord.* New York, 1972.

————. "A Summary of the Report by the Commission of Experts Appointed by H. E. Michele Cardinal Pellegrino, Archbishop of Turin." *Holy Shroud Guild Bulletin,* May 4, 1976.

————. "A Summary of the Critique of the Report of the Turin Commission on the Holy Shroud." Paper presented at The 1977 United States Conference of Research on the Shroud of Turin.

————. Taped personal conversations. 1973–77.

Roberts, C. H., and Turner, E. G., eds. *Catalogue of the Greek Papyri in the John Rylands Library, Manchester,* vol. 4. Manchester, 1952.

Robinson, John A. T. "The Shroud of Turin and the Grave Cloths of the Gospels." *Proceedings of the 1977 United States Conference of Research on the Shroud of Turin.* Colorado Springs, 1977, pp. 23–30.

————. Personal communication. May 10, 1977.

Rogers, Ray N. "Chemical Considerations Concerning the Shroud of Turin." *Proceedings of the 1977 United States Conference of Research on the Shroud of Turin.* Colorado Springs, 1977, pp. 131–35.

————. Personal communication. May 24, 1977.

Runciman, Steven. "Some Remarks on the Image of Edessa." *Cambridge Historical Journal* (1931): pp. 238–52.

Savio, P. "*Ricerche sopra la santa sindone.*" *Salesianum* 16 (1954): pp. 386–422, 622–77. *Ibid.*, 17 (1955): pp. 120–55, 319–90, 611–53. *Ibid.*, 18 (1956): pp. 578–640.

Smith, M. *Clement of Alexandria and a Secret Gospel of Mark*. Cambridge, Mass., 1973.

Sox, H. David. "Some Ecumenical Considerations Concerning the Turin Relic." *Proceedings of the 1977 United States Conference of Research on the Shroud of Turin*. Colorado Springs, 1977, pp. 16–19.

Strack, H. L., and Billerbeck, P. *Kommentar zum Neuen Testament aus Talmud und Midrasch*, vols. 1–4. Munich, 1922–28.

Thurston, H. "The Holy Shroud as a Scientific Problem." *The Month*, vol. 101 (1903): pp. 162–79.

————. "The Holy Shroud and the Verdict of History." *The Month*, vol. 101 (1903): pp. 17–29.

Tobler, T., et al., eds. *Itinera Hierosolymitana et descriptiones Terrae Sanctae Bellis Sacris Anteriora et Latina Lingua Exarata*, vols. 1 and 2. Geneva, (1) 1879, (2) 1885.

Tzaferis, V. "Jewish Tombs at and near Giv'at ha-Mivtar, Jerusalem." *Israel Exploration Journal*, vol. 20 (1970): pp. 18–32.

Vaccari, A. "*Recenti publicazioni sulla santa sindone.*" *Salesianum*, vol. 15 (1953): pp. 673–76.

Vignon, P. *The Shroud of Christ*. Translated from the French. Westminster, 1902.

————. *Le Saint Suaire de Turin devant la science, l'archéologie, l'histoire, l'incographie, la logique.* Paris, 1938.

Von Dobschuetz, E. *Christusbilder: Texte und Untersuchungen zur Geschichte der altchristlichen Li-*

teratur, edited by Gebhardt and Harnack, New Series, vol. 3, parts 1–4. Leipzig, 1899.

Walsh, John E. *The Shroud.* New York, 1963.

Webb, Charles. "Scientific Photography and the Shroud of Turin." Paper presented at The 1977 United States Conference of Research on the Shroud of Turin. Colorado Springs, 1977.

Willis, David. "Did He Die on the Cross?" *Ampleforth Journal* 74 (1969): pp. 1–13.

Wilson, Ian. "The Shroud's History Before the Fourteenth Century." *Proceedings of the 1977 United States Conference of Research on the Shroud of Turin.* Colorado Springs, 1977, pp. 31–49.

Wuenschel, Edward A. "The Holy Shroud of Turin: Eloquent Record of the Passion." *American Ecclesiastical Review,* vol. 93 (1935): pp. 441–72.

———. "The Holy Shroud. Present State of the Question." *American Ecclesiastical Review,* vol. 102 (1940): pp. 465–86.

———. "The Holy Shroud of Turin and the Burial of Christ." *Catholic Biblical Quarterly,* vol. 7 (1945): pp. 405–37.

———. "The Shroud of Turin and the Burial of Christ. Part II: John's Account of the Burial." *Catholic Biblical Quarterly,* vol. 8 (1946): pp. 135–78.

———. "The Truth about the Holy Shroud." *American Ecclesiastical Review,* vol. 129 (1953): pp. 3–19, 100–14, 170–87.

———. *Self-Portrait of Christ: The Holy Shroud of Turin.* Esopus, N.Y., 1954.